Afoot in the South:
Walks in the Natural Areas
of North Carolina

Afoot in the South:
Walks in the Natural Areas of North Carolina

Phillip Manning

Illustrations by Diane Manning

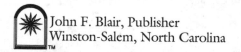

John F. Blair, Publisher
Winston-Salem, North Carolina

Book design by Debra Long Hampton
Illustrations by Diane Manning
Composition by The Roberts Group
Printed and bound by R.R. Donnelley & Sons

Library of Congress Cataloging-in-Publication Data

Manning, Phillip 1936–
    Afoot in the South : walks in the natural areas of North Carolina
    / Phillip Manning
        p.   cm.
    Includes index
    ISBN 0-89587-099-1 (trade pbk.)
    1. Natural History—North Carolina.   2. North Carolina—Description and
travel.   I. Title.
QH105.N8M36   1993
508.756—dc20   92-46868

To Steve Lee,
who taught Michael about willets

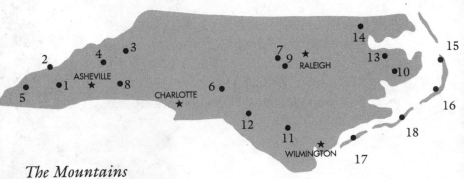

Contents

Acknowledgments

Without the contributions of Diane Manning, this book would not exist. She illustrated it, fearlessly critiqued and edited each draft, and accompanied me on most of the trips and many of the trails. It was, in fact, a joint effort.

The staff at John F. Blair, Publisher, was encouraging and demanding throughout the project. My special thanks go to Carolyn Sakowski, Steve Kirk, Margaret Couch, and Debbie Hampton. They are professionals.

A number of people contributed to the manuscript's final form. Dorrie Casey, Susan Ballinger, Mary Russell Roberson, Reece Schuler, and Maura Stokes listened well and commented intelligently every Monday night. Kelly Davis, Jim Ryan, Floyd Williams, and Al Carpenter vetted some of the chapters and straightened me out on several knotty issues. John Terres was kind enough to answer occasional questions and, in the process, teach me something about what being a naturalist means.

The most satisfying part of this project was meeting the men and women responsible for the on-site management of the natural areas of North Carolina. They were, without exception, dedicated, competent, and courteous. I, along with every other North Carolinian, am indebted to them for their hard work, sometimes under adverse circumstances. Without such people, our natural areas, if they existed at all, would be diminished. So please join me in thanking Bonnie Strawser, wildlife interpretive specialist at Pea Island National Wildlife Refuge; Bob Noffsinger, deputy manager of Pea Island National Wildlife Refuge; Walter Gravely, esteemed mapmaker and superintendent of South Mountains State Park; Allen Weakley, botanist for the North Carolina Natural Heritage Program; Sid Shearin, great nine-bean-soup chef and superintendent of Pettigrew State Park; Bill Davis, philosopher and maintenance supervisor at Jones Lake State Park; Michael Manning, full-time son and part-time historian of Bear Island, Hammocks Beach State Park; Ries Collier, biologist at Cape Hatteras National Seashore; Kelly Davis, writing stylist and biologist at Mattamuskeet National Wildlife Refuge; Judson Edeburn, Duke Forest manager, Duke University; Floyd Williams, chief ranger at Merchants Millpond State Park; Don Reuter, public-information officer for the North Carolina Division of Parks and Recreation; Jim Ryan, chief of resource planning for the Blue Ridge Parkway; Bob Miller, public-information officer at Great Smoky Mountains National Park; and Al Carpenter, senior geologist for the North Carolina Geological Survey.

Finally, though a great many people have helped in the preparation of this book, I alone am responsible for any omissions and errors that remain.

Introduction

And indeed, most of the Plantations in Carolina
*naturally enjoy a noble Prospect of large and spacious
Rivers, pleasant Savanna's, and fine Meadows, of most
glorious Colours, which the several Seasons afford; hedg'd
in with pleasant Groves of the ever-famous Tulip-tree, the
stately Laurel, and Bays, equalizing the Oaks in Bigness
and Growth; Myrtles, Jessamines, Wood-bines,
Honeysuckles, and several other fragrant Vines and Evergreens whose aspiring Branches shadow and interweave
themselves with the loftiest Timbers, yielding a pleasant
Prospect, Shade and Smell, proper Habitations for the
Sweet-singing Birds, that melodiously entertain such as
travel thro' the Woods of* Carolina.

John Lawson, 1709

I once had a job that required a great deal of travel. In ten
frenetic years, I visited every state—most of them many times. I
spent a lot of hours in airports and hotels and offices, but an
interest in the outdoors led me into the countryside whenever I
could get away. My main purpose was to relax and enjoy myself,
but I also wanted to learn something of the natural history of
the places in which I found myself. I quickly discovered that the
best way to do both was to find a spot to stretch my legs, a place
to take a long walk. But good walks were sometimes hard to

find, and I often wished for a guide that would help me locate them. For those who would like to learn about and enjoy the natural areas of North Carolina, this book is meant to be that guide.

More than five hundred miles long, with a landscape that rises from sea level to over a mile in altitude, North Carolina is a naturalist's dream. The state's Natural Heritage Program lists 104 distinct natural communities, from "Fraser Fir Forest" to "Salt Flat," from "Xeric Hardpan Forest" to "Low Pocosin."

Much of this diversity arises from the geography of the state. North Carolina consists of three physiographic regions—the mountains, the Piedmont, and the coastal plain—each of which is home to a variety of natural habitats. In this book, I have subdivided the coastal plain into two regions, adding the barrier islands as a separate province. This is not geologically correct, but this book is written primarily from a naturalist's point of view, and I believe that the natural communities found on the barrier islands are sufficiently different from those of the inner coastal plain to justify separating them.

Within each region, I have selected four or five walks—none of which requires backpacking—to illustrate some of the natural habitats of that region. The hardwood coves of Joyce Kilmer Memorial Forest are an example of one habitat in the mountain province, as the maritime evergreen forest of Buxton Woods is a habitat of the barrier islands. I make no claim of scientific methodology in selecting these walks. I merely tried to find the best trails through the most representative habitats of each region.

Many of the walks—like the "River Valley Walk" in the Smoky Mountains—were old friends, trails that I had walked many times before. But some—the walk entitled "A Flooded Forest" at Merchants Millpond, for example—were new to me. It was always a pleasure to discover a good walk in a new area, but there were disappointments, too. Croatan National Forest was one example. Though I went there many times, I was unable to find a good, long trail through its magnificent pine savannas. Nor could I come up with a walk that would do justice to the low pocosins of Alligator River National Wildlife Refuge. The successes and failures added up; in eighteen months, I walked more than three hundred miles in every region of the state. The walks selected for this book are the best of those miles.

Each chapter is composed of three parts and concerns itself with one walk. The first part consists of a map, a very brief description of the route, a mileage total for the walk, and an estimate of the degree of difficulty, whether easy, moderate, or strenuous. The second part tells something of the natural and cultural history of the area, and the third gives the hard information you will need to take the walk yourself—whom to write or call and where to stay, along with a bibliography.

For each walk, I have included enough information so that readers can easily follow my route, but I hope not so much that it will detract from the experience itself. One of the pleasures of a walk in a natural area is a degree of unpredictability. A good walk should be a mini-adventure, a change from the routines of everyday life. I believe these trails offer that requisite whiff of uncertainty.

In addition to the materials cited in the bibliographies attached to each chapter, I regularly consulted an array of Audubon Society and Peterson field guides which I have not listed. Four other books also proved to be valuable references, and since I used one or more of them in virtually every chapter, I chose not to include them in the chapter bibliographies. They were *North Carolina Hiking Trails*, second edition, by Allen de Hart; *A Directory to North Carolina's Natural Areas* by Charles E. Roe; *State Parks of North Carolina* by Walter C. Biggs, Jr., and James F. Parnell; and *Classification of the Natural Communities of North Carolina*, third approximation, by Michael P. Schafale and Alan S. Weakley.

Many of the trails in this book have been around for a while, and I hope that twenty-five or fifty or even a hundred years from now, walkers will be able to set out on the Appalachian Trail and walk from Clingmans Dome to Silers Bald. I hope that our sons and daughters can stroll beside the Eno River through the mellow hardwood forests that grow along its shores, and that coming generations will find Bear Island still untouched and natural.

For these things to be so, we must leave the land as we find it. And we must insist that others do the same. Most of these walks are on publicly owned land—our land. We must protect it from the careless, from the devious, from the kind of people for whom only the bottom line counts. If we don't, the land will vanish as surely as Glen Canyon slipped beneath the dammed waters of the Colorado River, and the natural communities will decline as certainly as the spruce-fir forest is disappearing from the pollution-shrouded peak of Mount Mitchell.

Most of these walks are on well-marked, well-mannered trails which are probably safer than the sidewalks of most cities. But some of them are in remote, isolated spots where you can still get lost or develop a blister or get caught in a sudden storm.

You can always twist an ankle or get bitten by mosquitoes or spiders or no-see-ums. So even though natural areas are not unusually dangerous places, it does make sense to take a few precautions.

Probably, the most straightforward way to stay safe in the woods, to keep inconvenience from turning into disaster, is to walk with someone. This is sensible advice, but for one reason or another, it is advice that I occasionally ignore. Sometimes, I can't find anyone who wants to go when I do, but more often, I prefer to walk alone, to see, hear, and smell the countryside on my own. Most of us spend our days surrounded by people, and a touch of solitude provides a respite from meetings and telephones and shopping malls.

But alone or with a companion, I always let someone know where I'm going and when I expect to be back. I also take a few safety-related items along in my haversack when I spend a day in the field:

map
compass
Band-Aids
pocketknife
Deet (for mosquitoes)
Skin-So-Soft (for no-see-ums)
full water bottle
matches
lightweight, waterproof windbreaker
clean, dry bandanna or handkerchief
aspirin or ibuprofen

Aside from the water, all of this gear weighs only a pound or two, and it costs less than a hundred dollars. And at one time or another, every item has proved useful.

Julian Price Memorial Park

THE MOUNTAINS

The Bears here are very common. . . . They sit by the Creeksides, (which are very narrow) where the Fish run in; and there they take them up, as fast as it's possible they can dip their Paws into the Water.

John Lawson, 1709

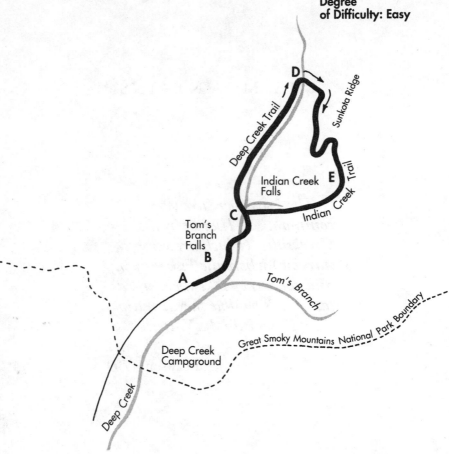

Length: 3.9 miles

**Degree
of Difficulty: Easy**

Deep Creek Trail

Sunkota Ridge

D

Indian Creek
Falls

E

Indian Creek Trail

C

Tom's
Branch
Falls

B

A

Tom's Branch

Great Smoky Mountains National Park Boundary

Deep Creek
Campground

Deep Creek

Deep Creek - Indian Creek Loop

A. Trailhead for
   Deep Creek - Indian Creek loop
B. Tom's Branch Falls
C. Southern intersection with
   Indian Creek loop
D. Northernmost point of
   Indian Creek loop
E. Begin Indian Creek jeep road

Route and Distances

A. to B.	0.4 mi.
B. to C.	0.5 mi.
C. to D.	1.0 mi.
D. to C.	1.1 mi.
C. to A.	0.9 mi.
TOTAL	3.9 mi.

River Valley Walk

Deep Creek–Indian Creek Loop
Great Smoky Mountains National Park

The trail starts at a gated fire road less than 0.25 mile north of Deep Creek Campground, which lies 3 miles north of Bryson City and just inside the border of Great Smoky Mountains National Park. For 2 miles, the trail parallels Deep Creek to an intersection with Indian Creek Trail. Proceed south on Indian Creek Trail across Sunkota Ridge to the Jeep road that follows Indian Creek back to Deep Creek. From there, it is 1 mile to the trailhead.

From its headwaters near the crest of the Smokies, Deep Creek runs south down the eastern flank of the mountains. By the time it reaches Deep Creek Campground, it's a lively, tumbling, sizable stream. Trout lie quietly in its cold, clear pools, and near the campground, laughing kids of summer fold themselves into oversized black inner tubes to bounce down its rapids. A creek adds an extra dimension to a walk, and since most of this loop is along boisterous Deep Creek or its tributary, Indian Creek, it is an especially agreeable way to explore the verdant lower ranges of the Smokies.

The high ridges of Great Smoky Mountains National Park can be rugged and austere, but the river valleys—like this one— are rounded and gentle, cloaked in a dense mantle of greenery.

This walk passes through a mixed forest of oak and maple, hemlock and poplar. Beneath the trees, tangles of blackberries, profusions of ferns, and thickets of laurel and rhododendron crowd one another, sucking nourishment from fertile black soil enriched by centuries of decayed vegetation. Life is abundant along Deep Creek, and its wildlife, wildflowers, and waterfalls make this walk special.

I've heard that in parts of Iowa the topsoil is so rich that if you sit quietly in a cornfield in midsummer, you can actually *hear* the corn grow. The valleys of the Smokies have that same fecund quality, and on the warm, drizzly morning in early summer when I take this walk, it isn't hard to imagine that the muted *snaps* and *pops* coming from the dripping green foliage are the sounds of growth, of trees heaving ever higher, of understory expanding beneath them, of seedlings pushing upward through forest duff.

A few hundred yards from the trailhead, Tom's Branch Falls cascades down a half-dozen steps into Deep Creek. A medium-sized bird with a distinct, slightly irregular wingbeat flies down the center of the creek. For a moment, the bird is between me and the falls, a wild, dark silhouette against the white water. It is a kingfisher, the first one I've ever seen at Deep Creek.

In fact, kingfishers are common in the Smokies in summer; they're just hard to see. They are easier to observe where the land is flatter and the trees sparser. The best kingfisher watching I know of is in southern Florida. Large numbers of these big-headed, heavy-billed birds perch on utility wires above the drainage canals along the Tamiami Trail, the highway that runs through the southern Everglades. They are grumpy-looking, solitary creatures, and each one maintains a distance of a quarter-mile or so from its neighbors. The spacing between birds is as regular as the telephone poles that line the road, and the unseen boundaries between perches define a territory, a segment of canal in which one bird alone has fishing rights. Those rights are crucial, since—as their name implies—these birds live almost exclusively on fish.

Kingfishers are distributed throughout the world, but only one species, the belted kingfisher (*Megaceryle alcyon*), is found in North Carolina. It is slightly larger than a robin, ash-blue on top and generally white underneath, with a blue band across its breast. A ragged crest tops its head, giving it a fierce, disheveled look. Its fishing technique is reminiscent of the pelican's, a momentary hover followed by a wings-back, beak-first, take-no-prisoners plunge. Fishing is what this bird was designed to do, and every part of its body is well suited to that task. In kingfishers, form does indeed follow function.

Beyond Tom's Branch Falls, the trail climbs gently, crisscrossing Deep Creek on wooden bridges. This is not one of the better-known walks in the Smokies, and though I am less than a mile from the crowds at Deep Creek Campground, the trail is deserted. Solitude can still be found in these mountains, and the quest for it has long attracted some men and a few women to the Smokies. Deep Creek was important in the life of one of those men, and his story makes the history of this valley every bit as interesting as the fauna and flora.

In 1911, Horace Kephart established a camp at Bryson Place, a few miles farther up Deep Creek. He hauled in his supplies in the spring over this trail and spent his summers here alone, occupying himself with camp chores and writing. During those years, he produced the classic book *Our Southern Highlanders*, a study of the mountaineers of the southern Appalachians, which is still in print nearly eighty years after it was first published.

Kephart had been a librarian in St. Louis until 1903, when, at age forty-one and in the throes of a monumental midlife crisis,

he re-created his life. He sent his wife and six children to live with her parents in New York, spent some time considering where to find the seclusion he craved, and, in 1904, lit out for the Smokies. He had a passion for wilderness, a weakness for booze, a keen eye, and—when sober—a sharp mind. Kephart died in an automobile accident in 1931 while returning home to Bryson City in a taxi after a visit to his bootlegger.

In addition to *Our Southern Highlanders*, Kephart wrote *Camping and Woodcraft*—a popular guide to wilderness living—several other books about the outdoors, and numerous articles for the sporting magazines of the day. He was called "the Dean of American Campers."

Kephart arrived in the Smokies just as large-scale logging was beginning there, and he spent much of the 1920s objecting to it. In article after article in newspapers and magazines, Kephart lent his support to the creation of a national park. Along with others, he saw the need to preserve these mountains as wilderness—even though they would no longer be wild enough to be his kind of wilderness. In a letter to his son concerning the government's purchase of the land that would become Great Smoky Mountains National Park, Kephart lamented, "Within two years we will have good roads into the Smokies, and then— well then I'll get out." He never had to get out, of course; the park wasn't officially dedicated until 1940, nine years after his death.

Horace Kephart is buried on a hilltop in Bryson City less than three miles from the Deep Creek trailhead. His headstone is a boulder, and from there, visitors can see wild, green mountains rising out of the mist. It is a view that Kephart would have surely appreciated.

There are numerous guides to the Smokies, and some of them mention the wildflowers one can expect to see along Deep Creek and Indian Creek, so as I walk, I make notes. My list for the day: ox-eye daisies, day lilies, phlox, flame azalea, blackberries (not blooming), wintergreen, and galax. After I finish the hike, I compare my list to that in one of the guides: strawberry bush, dog hobble, violets, Jack-in-the-pulpit, trillium, and Solomon's seal. The differences worry me. There's not a single flower in common. How did I miss the flowers that were supposed to be there? Did I misidentify the ones I saw?

That night, I pore over reference books, trying to—in the words of writer-naturalist Sue Hubbell—"organize my ignorance." After checking, I find that all of the plants I identified bloom in early summer, while those listed in the guides come to flower in spring. In just a month or two, there has been a 100-percent turnover in blooming wildflowers. Nature is never static, and wildflowers are particularly ephemeral, but the diversity of plant life in the Smokies dramatizes the seasonal changes, making them more obvious, and more vivid, than they are in the flatlands.

Near the end of the trail, I stop on a bridge just beyond Indian Creek Falls, a series of roily, whitewater waterfalls near the confluence of Indian Creek and Deep Creek. A good-sized brown trout is holding in a riffle below me. Kingfishers were once believed to eat small trout and were shot by fishermen who wanted to protect the fish. It turns out that kingfishers usually consume the sluggish chubs and suckers that live in the same waters. It also turns out that chubs and suckers eat trout eggs and trout fry. So, by killing kingfishers, the fishermen were inadvertently harming the very resource they were trying to protect.

As nature is not static, neither is it simple. Missing facts can lead one to doubt one's eyes about wildflowers or to reach a wrong conclusion about how to protect trout. In general, natural systems are too intricate to predict, too complex to manipulate. It is a fallacy to expect that pushing button A in an ecosystem will produce result B—and only result B. In fact, the unadvertised byproducts of such button pushing frequently turn out to be more important than the intended result.

If DDT had been advertised not as a pesticide but as a means of eliminating bald eagles, peregrine falcons, and brown pelicans from the East Coast, the product might have never been introduced. If Australians had known that the European rabbit would decimate the grasslands of their continent rather than just provide them with a little Old World hunting, they would likely have never let those cuddly balls of reproductive fluff off the boat. And if brown trout had not been introduced into North America from Germany in 1883, Deep Creek might still be filled with native brook trout, the browns' wilder and less-adaptable cousins, now found in the Smokies only in the highest, coldest streams.

But since brown trout grow larger than brookies, many fishermen prefer the European imports to native trout. In fact, the establishment of brown trout in North America is widely held to be one of man's more successful experiments in re-arranging nature. I'm not so certain, myself; brookies are colorful, elegant fish with a fierce, uncompromising quality about them that the more sophisticated browns don't have.

But Deep Creek harbors wildlife and wildflowers of all sorts—native and introduced—and pushing buttons in this park to rid it of non-native species, as a few nostalgic purists have suggested, would be foolhardy. The daisies along the trail, for example, also came from Europe. And like the sleek brown trout finning lazily in the clear water of Indian Creek, they seem very much at home in this fertile and complex ecosystem.

Before You Go

For More Information _____
Great Smoky Mountains National Park
Gatlinburg, Tenn. 37738
(615) 436-5615

Accommodations _____
Swain County Chamber of Commerce
P.O. Box 509
Bryson City, N.C. 28713
(704) 488-3681

Campgrounds _____
   Deep Creek Campground, 3 miles north of Bryson City, features over one hundred campsites set along the banks of Deep Creek.

Maps _____
   The trails are well marked, and the trail map that the park hands out free to visitors is all you'll need for this walk. If you are planning longer walks in the area, I suggest using topographic maps (USGS: Bryson City, Clingmans Dome).

Special Precautions _____

Great Smoky Mountains National Park is our nation's most-visited park. See the next walk, "The Appalachian Trail," for tips on how to avoid the summer-weekend crowds.

Additional Reading

The Alien Animals by George Laycock, Natural History Press, Garden City, N.Y., 1966.

Hiking in the Great Smokies by Carson Brewer, Holston Printing Company, Knoxville, Tenn., 1962. See "The Appalachian Trail" for my comments on this fine guide to day hiking in the Smokies.

Life Histories of North American Cuckoos, Goatsuckers, Hummingbirds, and Their Allies by Arthur Cleveland Bent, Dover Publications, New York, 1964. This book was originally published as *Bulletin 176* by the Smithsonian Institution in 1940.

Our Southern Highlanders by Horace Kephart, University of Tennessee Press, Knoxville, 1976. This reissue is a slightly revised reprint of the 1913 edition of Kephart's book. It also contains a mini-biography of Kephart written by George Ellison.

Strangers in High Places by Michael Frome, University of Tennessee Press, Knoxville, 1980. This is a revised edition of Frome's 1966 book, which was printed by Doubleday and Company.

Wildflowers of North Carolina by William S. Justice and C. Ritchie Bell, University of North Carolina Press, Chapel Hill, 1968.

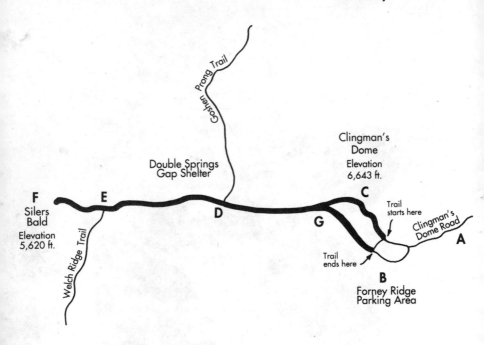

Length: 10.1 miles

**Degree
of Difficulty: Strenuous**

Goshen Prong Trail

Double Springs
Gap Shelter

Clingman's
Dome
Elevation
6,643 ft.

Trail
starts here

Clingman's
Dome Road

A

C

D

E

F
Silers
Bald
Elevation
5,620 ft.

Welch Ridge Trail

G

Trail
ends here

B
Forney Ridge
Parking Area

The Appalachian Trail

A. Clingman's Dome Road
B. Forney Ridge Parking Area
C. Clingman's Dome
D. Junction with Goshen Prong Trail
E. Junction with Welch Ridge Trail
F. Silers Bald
G. Exit to Forney Ridge Parking Area

Route and Distances

B. to C.	0.5 mi.
C. to D.	2.8 mi.
D. to E.	1.3 mi.
E. to F.	0.4 mi.
F. to G.	4.2 mi.
G. to B.	0.9 mi.
TOTAL	10.1 mi.

The Appalachian Trail

Clingmans Dome–Silers Bald
Great Smoky Mountains National Park

U.S. 441 is the only highway through the Smokies. At Newfound Gap, take Clingmans Dome Road to the Forney Ridge parking area. A paved path starts from the north side of the parking lot and leads 0.5 mile to the top of Clingmans Dome, where it intersects with the Appalachian Trail. Take the Appalachian Trail west for 4.5 miles to Silers Bald. Return the same way, except take the signed shortcut that begins 0.3 mile west of Clingmans Dome. The shortcut leads 0.9 mile back to the parking area.

*E*very time I take this walk, I swear "Never again!" The trail starts near Clingmans Dome in the highest parking lot in Great Smoky Mountains National Park. From there, it is five miles to Silers Bald. The walk there is easy, but the five miles back will get you, particularly the last three, which are uphill. Most of the trail is a mile high. Maybe it's the thin air, or perhaps the last stiff climb, but this walk always seems a mile too long. What draws me back is the trail itself, for nine of this walk's ten miles are on the most storied of all American footpaths, the Appalachian Trail.

How Benton MacKaye's dream became a 2,100-mile trail running between Springer Mountain, Georgia, and Mount Katahdin, Maine, is a well-known story. Its genesis was MacKaye's 1921 article, "An Appalachian Trail, A Project in Regional Planning," which appeared in the *Journal* of the American Institute of Architects. The idea of a long trail down the spine of the Appalachians caught on quickly. Within two years, the first section, a six-mile segment in New York, was completed, and by 1937, an Appalachian Trail was in place.

Since then, the trail has attracted millions of hikers, and not a few thrill seekers and record setters. In 1948, Earl Shaffer became the first "through hiker" by walking from Georgia to Maine in one trip. Emma Gatewood was the first woman to accomplish the feat, finishing on Mount Katahdin in September 1955. After that, the records began to get a little strange: the first dog, the first jogger, the first teenager, and so forth. Difficult feats, certainly, but it wasn't until 1990 that a "first" came along that impressed me. In that year, Bill Irwin of Burlington, North Carolina, and his dog, Orient, started the trail in March and finished it in November. The trip took longer than most through hikes because Bill Irwin is blind.

Irwin's eight-month trek to Maine struck me as a remarkable triumph, and he is on my mind the morning of my walk to Silers Bald. It is a cool day in early October, and the clusters of red berries on the mountain ashes are so bright they seem to burn a hole in the blue, cloudless sky. Mountain ash—or rowan tree—is a tree of the northern woods. Naturalist Donald Peattie says that it "reaches its greatest perfection north of Lakes Huron and Superior." It's a pipsqueak of a tree, rarely reaching thirty feet in height, and so scarce in this state that it is not described in *Common Forest Trees of North Carolina*. This far south, mountain ash is found only on the highest peaks. It may go unnoticed except in the late spring, when its showy white flowers cheer the gloomy spruce-fir forests, and in the fall, when its leaves turn to gold and its great clumps of berries stand out so clearly against the autumn sky. At those times, mountain ash is unmistakable, a tree to be commemorated. Some say that

Roan Mountain—an important landmark on the North Caro-lina–Tennessee border—got its name from the rowan trees near its summit.

The first leg of this hike is a half-mile walk on the steep, paved path up Clingmans Dome. I puff my way to the top, to the intersection with the Appalachian Trail. The altitude here is 6,643 feet, the highest point on the entire Appalachian Trail. From here, everything is downhill.

So that's the way I go, descending the white-blazed trail along a razorback ridge no wider than a nosebleed. I close my eyes for a second or two and nearly wind up on my fanny. How did Bill Irwin do it? The trail here isn't wide enough for a hiker and his dog to walk side by side. And it's rough; I'm constantly stepping on and over huge rocks, and roots reach up to trip me. Maybe I'll call and ask him when I get home.

The path continues—mostly downhill—through a long stretch of spruce-fir forest. Birds rustle in the trailside brush, and blackened ferns attest to a recent cold snap. At Double Springs Gap, a shelter for backpackers sits in an attractive grove of stubby, yellow-leaved trees. The altitude here is a thousand feet lower than at Clingmans Dome, and the preponderance of hardwoods reflects the gentler climate. A reddish-brown squir-rel sits at the base of one tree, working on a nut. When I walk toward him, he gives no ground and acts like he wants to duke it out with me. This behavior is typical of his breed, for this is not one of the common gray squirrels of suburbia but a red squirrel, *Tamiasciurus hudsonicus*, known in these parts as a "boomer."

Boomers are smaller than their more plentiful gray cousins. They are also more aggressive and, as their name implies, louder. As I close in on this one, he waits until the last second before scampering up a tree, then chatters noisily at my trespass. He leaves behind his nut, a slightly pitted husk encasing two large, shiny-brown kernels. They're buckeyes, the fruit of the golden trees that surround the shelter.

Yellow buckeyes (*Aesculus octandra*), sometimes called sweet buckeyes, are common in the rich mountain coves of the Smokies. Though the ones in this grove are stunted, buckeyes at lower elevations grow taller, sometimes reaching a hundred feet. Since the nuts are supposed to bring good luck, I stick one in my pocket for the walk back. Buckeye nuts are poisonous to livestock and humans, but apparently not to red squirrels, so I leave the other one for the boomer.

Not far beyond Double Springs Gap, yellow-leaved branches of beeches and buckeyes overhang the trail and create a golden tunnel through the forest. It's only a few hundred yards long, but it's a magical, spectacular section of trail, one that's hard to walk through (at least for me) without humming a bar or two of "Follow the Yellow Brick Road."

After the tunnel, the trail enters a moonscape filled with gnarled, barely living beech trees and the bleached crags of dead ones. At the Welch Ridge Trail intersection, the Appalachian Trail begins its final steep climb to Silers Bald. At the top, I drop my haversack, sprawl on the grass, and, with the sun warm on my face, remember another reason I enjoy this walk: grass balds are the best places in the world for a nap.

The Smokies are old, heavily forested mountains, but a few ridges and summits are treeless. These scalped areas are known as balds. Two types occur in this area—grass balds and heath balds. Heath balds are covered with azalea, laurel, and rhododendron; grass balds with, well, grass.

Ecologists have proposed more theories to explain the origin of grass balds than there are balds. They range from heavy grazing by domestic animals to soil acidity, from insect damage to "the effects of a previous xeric period." And though scientists seem to have a lot of fun thinking up new theories and arguing about them, no one knows for sure what caused balds to appear in these otherwise dense forests. Indians—who have been around these mountains a lot longer than scientists—told the early European settlers that their gods created them.

After my siesta, the first two miles of the walk back go quickly, but beyond Double Springs Gap, the inexorable uphill begins to take its toll. I stop to pant; stop to sit; stop to sit and pant. And that is how I happen to be parked on a rock by the side of the Appalachian Trail when the deer shows up.

White-tailed deer are common—pests, in fact—in the farms and fields of the southern Appalachians; they are often seen

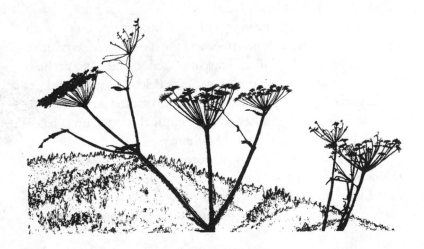

from cars as they feed on shrubs beside little-used mountain roads. But they are primarily creatures of the edge, finding their favorite browse in the region between forest and field. It's unusual to spot one in the deep woods.

This one is a fine, big doe, and her muscles move smoothly under a brown pelt that has a grayish cast in the dim forest light. She picks her way down the trail toward me, stopping occasionally for a nibble of this or that. She is less than ten yards away when she smells me. Her head jerks up and swivels around. I stare into two large, unafraid, liquid-brown deer eyes.

When I finally breathe, she takes two quick steps off the trail, putting a thin screen of green between us, and goes back to eating. I watch her for a few more minutes, then go back to walking. After a few paces, I stop to take one last look, but the doe has vanished.

The encounter with the deer energizes me and helps the trail fly by, but the final mile is as I remember it, a slow, stumbling nightmare of an uphill climb. For the umpteenth time, I ask myself how Bill Irwin did it. I promise to call and ask him if I ever get home.

In 1990, over three million men and women hiked some part of the Appalachian Trail, and eight million people visited Great Smoky Mountains National Park. The numbers give the impression that the Smokies section of the trail is a sidewalk filled rump-to-rump with hikers, a Fifth Avenue South with trees. But it's not. On that perfect-weather weekday, I saw nobody on my walk from Clingmans Dome to Silers Bald and passed only four people on the return. However, the number of hikers grows on the weekends, and except in winter, seekers of wilderness will find the traffic on the more popular trails uncomfortable—especially near the trailheads. But once you get two or three miles from the parking lots, the mobs thin out, and I, at least, have never felt crowded on any of the park's less-used trails. (See the "Before You Go" section for a list of trails to avoid on peak-season weekends.)

The reason, according to Bob Miller, a public-affairs officer at the park, is that 95 percent of the park's eight million visitors get no more than a few feet from their cars. In fact, 15 percent of them never get out of their cars at all. So Great Smoky Mountains National Park, the country's most-visited national park, winds up with traffic jams, packed parking lots, and many nearly deserted hiking trails.

"Hello," says the voice on the phone.

"Bill Irwin?" I ask.

"This is Bill."

I introduce myself, then get down to business. "I just finished a ten-mile walk on the Appalachian Trail. I'm sighted, and I'm tired. How did you do it?"

"God and Orient, my seeing-eye dog." The voice is slow, deliberate. "On some parts of the trail, I could only do four miles a day."

"Do you remember a particularly rough section in the Smokies? Between Silers Bald and Clingmans Dome?"

He pauses. "Well, I remember the Smokies. They were easy compared to what I found up north. I averaged sixteen miles a day in the park."

"The Smokies were easy?"

I guess he detects disappointment in my voice, because when he answers, I hear laughter in his. "Sure," Bill Irwin says. "It was like a sidewalk there."

"Sidewalk? Come on, Bill! Every time I closed my eyes—even for a second—to see what it was like for you, I almost fell. You walked the entire trail like that. How?"

"I fell," he says quietly. "A lot."

I hesitate before asking the next question, but I want to know. "How much is a lot?"

When he answers, I hear the steel and determination that pushed him 2,100 miles to the summit of Mount Katahdin and his moment of triumph. "I don't know for sure," he says. "Maybe five thousand times."

I thank Bill Irwin for his time and wish him good luck. Then I pick up the buckeye from my desk and rub it hard.

Before You Go

For More Information _____
Great Smoky Mountains National Park
Gatlinburg, Tenn. 37738
(615) 436-5615

Accommodations _____
Cherokee, Bryson City, and Gatlinburg all offer lodgings of every sort.
Cherokee Tribal Travel and Promotion
P.O. Box 460
Cherokee, N.C. 28719

(800) 438-1601

Swain County Chamber of Commerce
P.O. Box 509
Bryson City, N.C. 28713
(704) 488-3681

Gatlinburg Chamber of Commerce
P.O. Box 527
Gatlinburg, Tenn. 37738
(800) 822-1998

Campgrounds

In Great Smoky Mountains National Park, Smokemont and Elkmont campgrounds are closest to Clingmans Dome. Both are large campgrounds with splendid campsites.

Maps

The trails are well marked, and the trail map that the park hands out free to visitors is all you'll need for this walk.

Special Precautions

During weekends in the summer and in October, the roads and the most popular trails in the Smokies get crowded—particularly in the afternoons. According to public-affairs officer Bob Miller, Mount LeConte/Alum Cave Bluffs, Laurel Falls, Abrams Falls, the Chimney Tops, and Charlies Bunion are the trails solitude seekers might want to avoid during peak periods.

Additional Reading

The Appalachian Trail by Ann and Myron Sutton, J. B. Lippincott Company, Philadelphia and New York, 1967.

The Appalachian Trail by Ronald M. Fisher, National Geographic Society, Washington, D.C., 1972.

Common Forest Trees of North Carolina, 15th ed., originally prepared by J. S. Holmes, North Carolina Department of Natural Resources, Division of Forest Products, Raleigh, 1983.

"The Ecology of the Southern Appalachian Grass Balds" by A. F. Mark, *Ecological Monographs* 28, October 1958, 293–336.

Hiking in the Great Smokies by Carson Brewer, Holston Printing Company, Knoxville, Tenn., 1962. I've never seen this book for sale anywhere except in the park's visitor centers. It was the first and is still, to me, the best book on day hiking in the Smokies. I bought my first copy in 1963 for $1.00, and during my last visit, I noticed that it was still for sale. It's in its thirteenth printing, and the price is up to $2.85, but this unassuming little trail guide is still the best buy around.

Mammals of the Carolinas, Virginia, and Maryland by William David Webster, James F. Parnell, and Walter C. Biggs, Jr., University of North Carolina Press, Chapel Hill, 1985.

A Natural History of Trees of Eastern and Central North America by Donald Culross Peattie, Houghton Mifflin Company, Boston, 1948.

Length: 5.1 miles

**Degree
of Difficulty: Easy**

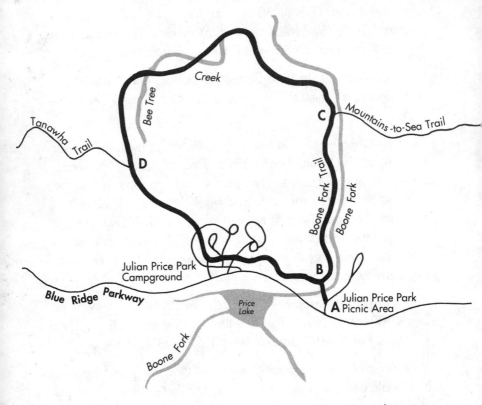

Boone Fork Trail

A. Julian Price Park picnic area
B. Trailhead for Boone Fork Trail
C. Junction with
   Mountains-to-Sea Trail
D. Junction with Tanawha Trail
   (part of Mountains-to-Sea Trail)

Route and Distances

A. to B.	0.1 mi.
B. to C.	1.1 mi.
C. to D.	2.7 mi.
D. to B.	1.1 mi.
B. to A.	0.1 mi.
TOTAL	5.1 mi.

A Green and Pleasant Land

Boone Fork Trail
Blue Ridge Parkway

The picnic grounds at Julian Price Memorial Park are located at Milepost 296.5 on the Blue Ridge Parkway. From the picnic area, a wooden footbridge leads west across Boone Fork to the signed trailhead less than 100 yards from the bridge. For a counterclockwise loop, proceed north along the western bank of Boone Fork. Halfway around the loop, the trail leaves Boone Fork and begins to generally parallel Bee Tree Creek. The path crisscrosses the creek, but rustic wooden bridges or strategically placed steppingstones make the crossings easy. After leaving Bee Tree Creek, the trail passes through a stile into a meadow. A footpath through the meadow leads to Julian Price Campground and continues back to the trailhead.

he Blue Ridge Parkway follows the crest of the Blue Ridge for 469 miles between Shenandoah National Park in Virginia and Great Smoky Mountains National Park in North Carolina. On my map, the parkway looks like a skinny green snake with bulges in it. The bulges indicate recreational areas, and the one near Milepost 295, a few miles northwest of Blowing Rock, is Julian Price Memorial Park. A campground and a picnic area occupy its center, and three well-marked trails squiggle off in various directions. The longest of the three is Boone Fork Trail, and it has been a favorite of mine for many years.

The 4,200-acre memorial park was donated to the National Park Service by Jefferson Standard Life, the Greensboro, North Carolina, insurance company that Julian Price ran for many years. The trail map the park service hands out has Price's photograph on the front. After years of walking these trails with the map and Julian Price's picture in my pocket, I feel like I know the man. If he were still alive, I'd like to get him away from his office and his appointments one morning to walk Boone Fork Trail with me. I'd like to see the resolute face in the photograph relax. I've come to believe that he might enjoy the walk.

It is an easy trail, with short and gentle slopes, that passes through bog, pasture, and rhododendron-filled forest. You are rarely out of earshot of the babble of Boone Fork or the murmur of Bee Tree Creek, and the air has a sharp, clean smell that tells you that you're in the southern Appalachians better than any map. There are no spectacular vistas along the way to make you gasp and no great physical challenges to overcome. It is simply a pleasant trail through a green and pleasant land.

I begin on a cool, misty morning in early October. After a few hundred yards, the trail passes through a boggy area that was once a lake bed. By the time I cross the bog, I can tell that the crowds which will flood the parkway during the next three weeks will be disappointed: this will not be a vintage year for fall colors. Maple leaves, which ordinarily transform the trees into fiery red torches by the middle of the month, have already fallen, and they cover the path with the colors of a subdued fall, a fading green freckled with brown.

The trees near the bog and along Boone Fork are not sugar maples (*Acer saccharum*), although those magnificent trees of New England can be found in these mountains. These are red maples (*Acer rubrum*), and it is not surprising to find them near water, for the red maple is also known as swamp maple.

Unlike the sugar maple, which occurs naturally in North Carolina only in the mountains, the red maple thrives throughout the state and can be found as far south as Florida. And if the tree lacks the patrician image of its slightly larger, maple-syrup-producing cousin, the red maple is still a handsome tree, with a diamond-shaped crown that can reach heights of one hundred feet. It produces red buds in winter that become tiny red flowers in early spring, and even in midsummer its leafstalks are autumnal red. But the red maple reaches its colorful peak in the fall, when its leaves light up the woods with their brilliant scarlet hue.

Or at least they usually do. Along the parkway this year, something has suppressed the red maple's usual flame, giving leaf aficionados a chance to indulge in their second most pleasurable pastime—speculating as to what that something is. Too wet for much color, one grumbles; too hot, another says. The problem is a dry fall combined with a cool summer, a third chimes in. Who knows? To me, the greens and the browns and the sprinkling of reds are quietly beautiful. The crimsons, the oranges, and the shining yellows will be back next season, and the year-to-year comparison will make them seem all the more dazzling.

Beyond the bog, the trail continues along Boone Fork, and tulip poplars, beeches, and yellow birches replace the swamp maples. Along this section of trail, the understory is mostly rhododendron, mountain laurel, and flame azalea. These shrubs show only dark green now, but come spring, the trail will blaze with blossoms of white, pink, and outrageous orange.

I stop several times to watch and listen to Boone Fork. Near the trailhead, it is just another pretty, piddling mountain stream, but the farther downstream you go, the mightier it becomes. And by the time you reach the halfway point in the walk, near the spot where the trail diverges from Boone Fork, this once-gentle creek has become a full-fledged whitewater river filled with car-sized boulders.

Soon afterward, as the trail starts to climb, following Bee Tree Creek back toward the parkway, I see a twitch of gray scratching in the underbrush. A junco, a common bird in the southern Appalachians, is hunting and pecking among the leaves on the forest floor.

Juncos are small gray birds closely related to sparrows. They are found throughout the eastern United States—often on the ground beneath backyard bird feeders searching for stray seeds. Perhaps because of the species' widespread distribution, birders have a lot of names for *Junco hyemalis*, including slate-colored junco, white-winged junco, dark-eyed junco, and Northern junco. Because these birds usually migrate to North Carolina in the winter, local birders often refer to them as snowbirds. At one time, the nonmigratory junco found in these mountains was thought to be a separate subspecies called the Carolina junco.

Today, in a pleasant reversal of the usual trend, the birds abound, but some of the names have become extinct. Now, the species is almost always referred to as the dark-eyed junco. But if you see one pecking at the ice on a wintry day, no one will mind if you slip up and call it a snowbird.

The trail continues gently upward, skipping back and forth across Bee Tree Creek through a second-growth hardwood forest. These hills were logged as late as 1930, and the forest has yet to recover its former grandeur. Some of the logs hauled out of here were six to eight feet in diameter and well over two hundred years old. And it's going to take at least that much time for the trees to reach that size again.

Of course, grandeur is just a word some people assign to old-growth forests, and where one person sees grandeur, another sees a meal ticket. Both points of view are valid, depending upon the state of your stomach. The problem is that if you don't log a forest, you can always change your mind and come back and cut it the next day or the next week or the next year. But if you do log a forest, only time, and a lot of it, will bring the trees back. One decision is reversible; the other is not. One decision conserves the land for future generations which may hunger more for forests than for lumber; the other denudes it today without regard for the future.

The last leg of the walk winds through a meadow and a campground. There are chipmunks and bulls, crows and cow patties, and kids playing tag. There are campfires and tents and picnic tables. People move lazily about their campsites or sit and stare dreamily at their fires. The air smells of smoldering charcoal and grilling hamburgers. I welcome the noise and the whiff of civilization after the quiet solitude of the woods, but I wonder what Julian Price would have thought about this campground, about this leisure, about all this *wasted* time.

I pull the black-and-white photograph out of my pocket. In it, Price is outdoors, standing at the bottom of a stone stairway somewhere in the mountains. He is a compact man, dressed in a dark suit, white shirt, and dark tie. He is wearing a hat and holding a cane in his right hand. He is not smiling and appears to be looking at something far off. I think I see sadness in his face, a look of loss masked by sternness. The brochure describes

him as a "self-made man in the best American tradition."

He was certainly that. A gushy magazine article published shortly after he died was titled "Julian Price: From Railroad Telegrapher to Life Insurance Company Presidency." Price became president of Jefferson Standard in 1919, at age fifty-one. It was a small company then, but by the time he turned the job over to his son just a few months before his death in 1946, its assets had grown to nearly $175 million.

The magazine article states that Price was a joiner, and it lists a dozen or so civic and social organizations to which he belonged. Although he rarely played golf, he was a member of three country clubs. Julian Price, the article says, was an energetic man, a man who was never idle, one who hated laziness. "A lazy man," he is quoted as saying, "every day you keep him, you're throwing your money away." I suspect he was not the sort of man who would have indulged in campfire staring—or approved of it, either.

But what about the regret, the sense of loss I think I see in the photograph? Maybe I'm making too much of a single picture. Perhaps his breakfast didn't agree with him. But later, I find more old photos. In each of them, Julian Price wears exactly the same expression.

Price farmed the land that Jefferson Standard later donated to the National Park Service, the land that became Julian Price Memorial Park. Not personally, of course—he was too busy for that. Seven families lived on the property and raised cows and pigs and sheep and other things that interested the owner. According to the magazine article, Price intended to retire there "when he got old."

But he was a month shy of his seventy-ninth birthday when

he died in an automobile accident, and he never got around to retiring, probably never got to spend much time in these green hills, probably never got to walk Boone Fork Trail on a cool October morning—except as a passenger in a stranger's pocket. He probably never got to spend much time at anything but building one of the larger life-insurance companies in the South. And that might be the source of the regret I think I see in the photograph. Although Price loved his job, he may have realized that his dedication to business had cost him something. Perhaps when he was young he made an important decision about how he intended to lead his life, only to discover later that some decisions, like the clear-cutting of old-growth forests, are irreversible.

Before You Go

For More Information _____

For general information about the parkway, contact the headquarters office:

Blue Ridge Parkway
200 B.B.& T. Building
One Pack Square
Asheville, N.C. 28801
(704) 259-0701

Eleven ranger offices are spaced along the parkway. For detailed information about Julian Price Memorial Park, contact

Sandy Flats Office
Route 1, Box 565
Blowing Rock, N.C. 28605
(704) 295-7591

Accommodations

Motels are available in Blowing Rock and Boone. For information, contact
Blowing Rock Chamber of Commerce
Box 406
Blowing Rock, N.C. 28605
(704) 295-7951

Boone Area Chamber of Commerce
827 Blowing Rock Road
Boone, N.C. 28607
(704) 264-2225

Campgrounds

The 197 campsites at Julian Price Memorial Park (Milepost 296.9) are clean and well maintained. The campground is open all year except during periods of severe winter weather.

Maps

The map in the brochure that the National Park Service gives out free to visitors is adequate for this well-marked trail.

Additional Reading

Birds of North Carolina by Thomas Gilbert Pearson, Clement Samuel Brimley, and Herbert Hutchinson Brimley, revised by David L. Ray and Harry T. Davis, North Carolina Department of Agriculture, State Museum Division, Raleigh, 1959.

Blue Ridge Parkway Guide, Book 3, *Boone-Blowing Rock-Asheville* by William G. Lord, Hexagon Company, Asheville, N.C., 1976.

"Julian Price: From Railroad Telegrapher to Life Insurance Company Presidency" by Lou Rogers, *We the People 4*, December 1946, 22–25.

A Natural History of Trees of Eastern and Central North America by Donald Culross Peattie, Houghton Mifflin Company, Boston, 1948.

Walking the Blue Ridge by Leonard M. Atkins, University of North Carolina Press, Chapel Hill, 1991.

Length: 5.6 miles (one-way)

**Degree
of Difficulty: Moderate to Strenuous**

Mount Mitchell State Park

Pisgah National Forest

BLACK MOUNTAINS

**MOUNT
MITCHELL**

Elevation
6684 ft. **B**

Camp
Alice

Mt. Mitchell Trail

Higgins Bald Trail

Higgins
Bald

Black Mountain
Campground

A Elevation
3000 ft.

South Toe River

Mount Mitchell Trail

A. Black Mountain Campground
B. Summit of Mount Mitchell

Route and Distances

A. to B.   5.6 mi.

TOTAL   5.6 mi.

The Spruce-Fir Forest

Mount Mitchell Trail
Pisgah National Forest and Mount Mitchell State Park

Black Mountain Campground is located on Forest Road 472 off N.C. 80. From the auxiliary parking lot at the campground, take Briar Bottom Road toward the group campsite. The blue-blazed Mount Mitchell Trail starts 0.25 mile from the campground and climbs north via a series of well-graded switchbacks. After 1.5 miles, the switchbacks vanish, and Higgins Bald Trail splits off to the left. Continue right on Mount Mitchell Trail. At mile 2.7, the two trails merge again. From there, it is another 1.2 miles to the junction with Buncombe Horse Range Trail. Bear left on the horse trail. After 0.1 mile, Mount Mitchell Trail splits off to the right for the last 1.6-mile slog to the summit. Since this is a one-way walk, you will need to prearrange transportation back down to your car.

I've heard experienced hikers say that walking up a mountain is easier than walking down. After climbing Mount Mitchell, the highest mountain east of the Mississippi River, you'll either decide never to walk down it, or you'll conclude that experienced hikers have goofy ideas. In less than six miles, from Black Mountain Campground in Pisgah National Forest to the summit in Mount Mitchell State Park, Mount Mitchell Trail rises nearly 3,700 feet, over two-thirds of a mile. Walking this trail is the vertical equivalent of climbing to the top of the Empire State Building three times—except, of course, there are no stairs on Mount Mitchell.

But the trail is short, and even if you stop to rest along the way, a moderately fit person can make it easily in half a day. And there's a lot to see and think about while you're climbing, for few wild areas have played as prominent a role in the cultural and natural history of North Carolina as Mount Mitchell.

About thirty miles northeast of Asheville, a ridge of dark mountains rises out of the green valleys. These are the Black Mountains, named for the somber spruce-fir forests that cap them. Black Mountain Campground lies east of these mountains, and by the time I arrive, campers are busying themselves with breakfast. I smell coffee and bacon and wood smoke and hear the chattering of jays and squirrels as I stroll through the campground to the trailhead. It's a cool midsummer morning.

The first mile of trail consists of a series of switchbacks, a civilized, blue-blazed, well-maintained path rising through a hardwood forest. I am not fooled; I've walked this trail before, and I know what's coming. Although I'm not tired, I stop to rest after a couple of miles.

The United States Forest Service rates the use of this trail as heavy, but I have seen no other hikers, and the spider webs in my hair tell me that I'm the first person to walk it today. As I listen to crows calling in the distance, I consider this mountain and what it must have been like in the early years of our country. There were no trails then, and the individual peaks had no names. Back then, they were collectively called the Black

Mountain.

French botanist André Michaux was the first European to explore the range. In 1789, he left Turkey Cove for the Blacks, about twenty-five miles away. He was gone for six days. It is not clear what route he took, or how far he ascended, but something he saw impressed him, because he returned a few months later to climb in these mountains again. Historians think that his second journey took him up the eastern slope of the Blacks, above the South Toe River, approximately the route I'm following today. It is unlikely, I think, that he stopped and rested after two short miles. After all, he covered fifty miles in six days and spent most of his time collecting samples. I start walking again.

The path is wet and muddy, overrun with mountain laurel and rhododendron. Indian pipes grow beside the trail, and a few small evergreens appear among the hardwoods, the first sign of the spruce-fir forest that dominates at higher elevations. In 1794, Michaux made his last trip to *la Montagne Noire*. He returned with a sample of red spruce. In the Blacks, red spruce are found at altitudes of four thousand feet and higher, but they are most common between five and six thousand feet. Below five thousand feet, hardwoods predominate, and above six thousand, the Fraser fir is supreme. Since Michaux collected no samples of the latter, it is unlikely he made it to the peaks, and he recorded no mention of reaching the crest of the range in his journals. The first man to make that claim, Elisha Mitchell, didn't come along until a generation later.

Mitchell came to North Carolina from Connecticut, bringing with him a diploma from Yale and a Puritan heritage that went back many years. He arrived at the tiny village of Chapel

Hill in January 1818 to teach mathematics and natural philosophy at the University of North Carolina, a school which consisted of three buildings and 120 students at that time. Though the town and school must have seemed primitive to him, Mitchell settled in quickly.

During the next few years, he taught his classes, got married, and set about completing an agricultural and geological survey of the state. In an unpublished biography, Mitchell's daughter quotes her father as saying that "whatever portion of my time is not occupied by my duties at the University . . . will be zealously devoted to the geology and mineralogy of the State." Elisha Mitchell had found his mission, and he began to prowl his adopted state, measuring and recording with puritanical fervor.

As head of the North Carolina Geologic Survey, Mitchell visited all of the state's geographic regions. In the summer of 1827, he explored the country west of the Blue Ridge. On that trip, he got his first glimpse of the Blacks. At the time, Mitchell

must have thought there was something special about them, a loftiness that set them apart, for he returned a year later to visually compare their height to that of other mountains in the area. By 1835, he wanted to know exactly how tall these mountains were. That summer, he set out to measure them.

To do so, he had to get to the top of the Blacks, and the trail I am walking reminds me that that was no piece of cake. The path has narrowed to a few inches as it passes through a dense, shadowy rhododendron thicket, and even after it widens and enters the spruce-fir forest, it is still dark and damp and forever uphill. How did Mitchell manage this climb when there were no trails, no friendly forest-service blazes, no switchbacks? In his journals, he described one ascent as "the hardest day's work I ever performed." He characterized his path as a "burrow above ground" and implied that he, like the bears, had to proceed on all fours. As I walk, that sinks in. He crawled up the mountain on a *bear trail*?

The trail crosses a small creek, and I tiptoe across it on well-placed steppingstones. A mini-waterfall spills down a slab of rock just upstream. It's rough country, but it's also cool and quiet. Mitchell said it would be "a comfortable place to die in." Of course, he had no intention of doing so; all he wanted to do was measure the height of that Black Mountain.

To accomplish the task, he took with him two mercury barometers. You may remember them from high school. A U-shaped glass tube, with one end closed off and the other open to the atmosphere, is filled with mercury and clamped to a board, with a yardstick placed vertically between the arms of the U. At sea level, the pressure of the atmosphere will raise the mercury in the sealed tube about thirty inches above its level in the open column. As you climb above sea level, atmospheric pressure decreases, and the column of mercury it will support also decreases. At a mile above sea level, a mercury barometer will read only a little over twenty-four inches; at the altitude of most jet flights, it will read less than eight inches.

To correct for normal fluctuations in pressure due to weather, measurements must be averaged over a very long time, or else simultaneous readings must be made at a nearby site where the weather is the same and the altitude is known or can be measured. Mitchell, no fool, chose the latter method, selecting Morganton as his control site.

A Mr. Pearson was assigned to take the readings in Morganton. In his account of the trip, Mitchell said that "the mean of ten observations, on successive days, gave what is probably a near approximation to the height of Morganton above the level of the Sea—968 feet." While Pearson read his barometer in Morganton, Mitchell was taking his measurements in the mountains.

His first stop was Grandfather Mountain. After comparing his reading, taken at the top of the mountain, with those made the same day in Morganton, Mitchell calculated Grandfather's height to be 4,588 feet above Morganton. His next stop was Roan Mountain, 5,070 feet above Morganton, and his last was Black Mountain, where his barometer read 23.807 inches— 5,508 feet above Morganton, or 6,476 feet above sea level. Since Mount Washington, the country's highest mountain, was then thought to be 6,234 feet tall, Elisha Mitchell had just measured the highest peak yet found in the United States.

Of course, our country was smaller then. Today, Mount Mitchell is a pygmy compared to the towering peaks of Alaska and Hawaii, and the Black Mountains are dwarfed by the Rockies and the Sierras. But pygmy mountains or not, the path I'm following continues ever upward. Even today, climbing the Blacks is no Sunday stroll.

Suddenly, sunlight floods the trail as it crosses a ribbon of ground that has been cleared for electric lines. There are grasses and weeds and thistles with spiky purple flowers covered with butterflies. My eye follows the utility poles, hoping to see the summit, but the lines vanish into a depression. To reach the top, I know I must go uphill, but in which direction? From where I stand, there is no way of telling Mount Mitchell from the other peaks. Without the blue-blazed trail, I'd have little chance of ending up on it. This was the problem that came to haunt Mitchell. Which peak did he climb? Could he find it again and reproduce his measurements? Was it really the highest of the Blacks?

He began to have doubts in 1838 when he made a second trip to Black Mountain, this time ascending the range from a different direction. With this new perspective, he later became "fully satisfied that I was not upon the highest point in the Black Mountain ridge in 1835." He also learned that there may have been "considerable error in the elevation [I] assigned to Morganton." So, in 1844, he made a third trip, "determined to try the Black once more."

This time, Mitchell established his base in Asheville, leaving a friend there to take barometric readings. The now-paunchy fifty-year-old professor was not looking forward to climbing the Blacks again and said so in a letter to his wife. In the same letter, though, Mitchell broke some good news: "I did not think that the name Mitchell which some had affixed to . . . [one of the peaks in the Blacks] would adhere, but now I begin to think it will. When I stopped at Solomon Carter's on Friday night I asked a young fellow if the Black Mountain was visible from a neighboring hill. He replied that he could show me Mount Mitchell from there."

The professor had a mountain named for him. And now he hoped to find out how tall it *really* was.

The next day, Mitchell climbed the highest peak he could find, took his measurements, and after comparing them with readings made the same day in Asheville, pronounced the Black Mountain to be 6,672 feet tall, almost 200 feet taller than his original estimate. For the first time, Mitchell felt certain that he had reached the highest peak and confident that his measurements were accurate. He returned to Chapel Hill, published his findings, settled into the less-strenuous life of a respected professor, and put the Black Mountain behind him. Which, by the time I cover the next couple of miles and reach the Camp Alice Trail Shelter, is where I'd like to put it, too.

I'm tired, and it's another mile and a half to the summit. I can see buildings on the peaks in front of me, but I still can't see the tower that marks the top of Mount Mitchell. I cross an invisible line and leave Pisgah National Forest for Mount Mitchell State Park. The friendly blue blazes vanish, and a profusion of trails and logging roads greets me.

This is open country, grass-green and rocky, a reminder of the extensive logging that took place before Mount Mitchell became North Carolina's first state park in 1915. Butterflies—mostly swallowtails and blues—attack every wildflower still in bloom. The path I'm on splits and goes off in several directions. I still can't see the tower that tops Mount Mitchell, but instead of consulting the map, I head for the highest peak I can see. If Mitchell found the highest point in the Blacks without a map, surely I can, too. I've been here before, and I've got trails to follow and a tower to look for. (It is at this point, when I decide to go it without a map, that my path begins to deviate from the route up Mount Mitchell outlined at the beginning of this walk. Hikers are advised to follow the traditional route.)

Although Mitchell tried to forget the Black Mountain, it was not to be. In 1855, Thomas Clingman—a United States congressman from Asheville, a man with a strong interest in science, and a friend and former student of Mitchell's—took a trip to the Blacks. His purpose was to measure the altitudes of the highest peaks and to determine, once and for all, which was tallest.

The result was confusion. Was the tallest peak Clingman found the same one Mitchell had measured in 1844, the peak known officially by then as Mount Mitchell? Clingman said no; Mitchell said yes. The controversy grew testy. Articles were written; letters were exchanged. The tallest mountain was renamed Clingman's Peak. Another mountain, a shorter one, was officially designated Mount Mitchell. Elisha Mitchell and his mountain were now number two.

Mitchell returned to the Blacks in the summer of 1857, determined to confirm his 1844 measurements. He was sixty-four years old and overweight, but he felt his integrity and scientific reputation had been questioned. And there was enough Puritan spirit in him for one more ascent.

On the afternoon of June 27, he set off on foot from a lodge on the southern flank of the Blacks and headed into the mountains. He was never seen alive again. Eleven days later, a search party led by legendary mountain guide Big Tom Wilson found Elisha Mitchell's body face-down in a pool at the base of a forty-foot waterfall. His watch had stopped at 8:20.

I glance at mine. It's almost noon; I should have reached the summit by now. I'm pretty sure I'm on the wrong trail, but it's still going up and there are peaks in front of me. Stubbornly, I keep walking.

Finally, I see pavement ahead and a building with a Ford Bronco parked in front of it. It turns out to be the park office, nearly two miles south of Mount Mitchell. I sprawl wearily on the stairs. A ranger in a razor-sharp uniform with a huge pistol hanging from a heavy belt, a Smokey the Bear hat, and mirror sunglasses comes out of the office door. His expression is disapproving. He reminds me of the guard in *Cool Hand Luke*. But after I explain my situation, his face splits into a grin. "How about a lift?" he asks.

So I ride to the parking lot of the tallest mountain east of the Mississippi River in a Ford Bronco with sawed-off shotguns in the front and back seats, then walk the last few hundred yards to the summit. On top, there is an observation tower, a sign, and a grave. The grave is Elisha Mitchell's, and the sign says the elevation is 6,684 feet.

After his death, the public demanded that the name of the tallest mountain be changed from Clingman's Peak back to Mount Mitchell. It was, and the question of whether Mitchell ever really climbed it became a topic for historians to debate.

In view of Mitchell's routes and measurements and the testimony of his guides, the consensus today is that Mitchell didn't reach the top of the Blacks in 1844, as he so passionately believed. Instead, historians suspect he reached it in his first climb, in 1835. The evidence is not conclusive, but a simple calculation leads me to concur.

Based on Pearson's readings in 1835, Mitchell calculated the altitude of Morganton as 968 feet; his own measurements told him that the Black Mountain was 5,508 feet above that. We know today that Morganton is actually 1,182 feet above sea level. If Mitchell had known the correct altitude of Morganton, he would have come up with a height of 6,690 feet for the Black Mountain, only 6 feet higher than the altitude posted at the summit. Considering the crudeness of Mitchell's barometers, the closeness of these numbers may be coincidental, but it seems likely to me that Mitchell did indeed climb his mountain in 1835—and measure its height accurately.

Much has changed on the mountain since Mitchell's day. Although the dark green spruce-fir forest is still abundant along the trails, it has almost vanished from the summit, which looks more like a war zone than a park. Naked Fraser firs, dead and dying, stand craggy and gray on the slopes; windfalls have cleared large areas, and downed trees rot on the ground.

There have been studies of this devastation, along with a great deal of publicity. In the 1980s, the *New York Times*, "60 Minutes," and a raft of local publications did stories on the plight of Mount Mitchell. Many researchers believed air pollution was the culprit, but no one could prove it. Several facts are known:

Mount Mitchell is cloaked in clouds seven days out of ten, and in cold weather the moisture causes rime ice to form on the needles and branches of the trees. Since the summit was heavily logged early in this century, the ice-heavy trees are exposed to the full force of the storms that regularly rake the mountain in winter. The size of the windfalls appears to be expanding.

The concentration of nitrogen, sulfur, lead, and other pollutants in the clouds that bathe Mount Mitchell's summit is ten to one hundred times higher than the pollution found on an average downtown street in urban North Carolina. Since the trees near the peak spend 70 percent of their lives with their heads in those deadly fumes, most scientists believe air pollution is weakening them. Pollution has also been blamed for ravaging the spruce forests of New England and Europe.

In 1955, the first balsam woolly aphid was detected on Mount Mitchell. Aphids are small, soft-bodied, plant-sucking insects. Balsam woolly aphids attach themselves beneath the bark of Fraser firs—also called balsams. The trees respond by growing a very hard layer of wood, known as heartwood, to repel the tiny invaders. The heartwood restricts the trees' capacity to pump water to their canopies, causing the needles and eventually the entire tree to die. Red spruce are believed to be immune to the woolly aphid.

According to park rangers, Mount Mitchell has endured worse-than-usual winters in the last decade.

Combining these facts into a coherent theory that explains the devastation at the mountain's summit spawned a cottage industry that supported quite a few scientists for quite a few years. But the researchers reached no final conclusions.

It's likely that logging, bad weather, pollution, and aphids are all parts of the plague that is destroying this forest. It is also likely that pollution stresses trees already exposed by logging, weakening them and making them more vulnerable to bad weather and small bugs—even if it can't be proved. And since logging on the summit was stopped seventy-five years ago, pollution is the only one of the possible villains we can do much about.

When I hitched to the summit with the ranger, he warned me of the destruction there, attributing most of the damage to bad weather. As we rode, I asked him about the pollution studies that had been done and whether any work was under way to clean up the air at the top. "Everybody knows the air up here is bad," he said, "but nothing much is going on. We ran out of money. The scientists are into global warming now. They go where the money is."

I thought about Elisha Mitchell and his work on the mountain. "Not all of them," I said.

Before You Go

For More Information

United States Forest Service
Pisgah National Forest
Toecane Ranger District
Burnsville, N.C. 28714
(704) 682-6146

Mount Mitchell State Park
Route 5, Box 700
Burnsville, N.C. 28714
(704) 675-4611

Accommodations

Yancey County Chamber of Commerce
2 Town Square
Burnsville, N.C. 28714
(704) 682-7413

Campgrounds

Mount Mitchell State Park has nine tent-camping sites open from mid-May to mid-October. Black Mountain Campground is much larger and can accommodate trailers. The South Toe River runs through this campground, and if you camp there, its gentle, soporific gurgle will put you asleep faster than any pill.

Maps

The South Toe River Trail Map, available from the United States Forest Service for a small fee, covers the route from Black Mountain Campground to the park. The last mile of the trail is in Mount Mitchell State Park, and you will need the map in the park brochure to help you negotiate it. The profusion of trails in the park can be confusing, so pay attention.

Special Precautions

There are three ways to walk Mount Mitchell Trail: up, down, or round trip. For the first two, you'll need someone with a car to meet you at trail's end. I would rate the third hike as very strenuous, a walk suitable only for those in excellent physical condition.

Points of Interest

Mount Mitchell is just a few miles from the Blue Ridge Parkway via N.C. 128. Craggy Gardens, to the west, and Crabtree Meadows, to the east, have picnic areas, views, and hiking trails.

Additional Reading

Aphid Ecology by A. F. G. Dixon, Blackie and Son, Limited, Glasgow, Scotland, 1985.

"Biography of Elisha Mitchell" by Thomas L. Jones, honors thesis, University of North Carolina at Chapel Hill, 1973.

A History of Mt. Mitchell and the Black Mountains by S. Kent Schwarzkopf, North Carolina Division of Archives and History, Raleigh, 1985. I drew heavily on this book for its accounts of Mitchell's climbs in the Black Mountains.

"Trouble on Mount Mitchell" by Lawrence S. Earley, *Wildlife in North Carolina* 48, December 1984, 11–17.

Visitors to the Black Mountains might also be interested in Elisha Mitchell's article "The Mountains of Carolina," which appeared in the *Raleigh Register* on November 3, 1835.

Length: 4.2 miles

**Degree
of Difficulty: Easy**

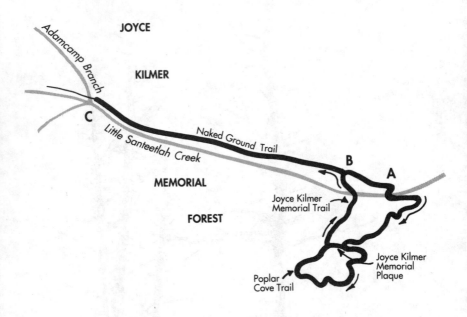

Joyce Kilmer - Naked Ground Trails

A. Joyce Kilmer Memorial Forest
   picnic area and parking lot
B. Intersection of Joyce Kilmer loop
   with Naked Ground Trail
C. Confluence of Adamcamp Branch
   and Little Santeetlah Creek

Route and Distances

A. to B.	Joyce Kilmer double loop	1.8 mi.
B. to C.	Naked Ground Trail	1.1 mi.
C. to A.	Return to parking lot	1.3 mi.
	TOTAL	4.2 mi.

An Old-Growth Hardwood Cove

Joyce Kilmer–Slickrock Wilderness
Nantahala National Forest

From Robbinsville, go north on U.S. 129 for 1 mile and follow the signs to the Joyce Kilmer Wilderness Area. The trailhead is a few feet from the parking lot. The 2-mile Joyce Kilmer National Recreation Trail is a double-loop trail shaped like a figure eight. The first loop is Joyce Kilmer Memorial Trail; the second is Poplar Cove Trail. If you walk the loops clockwise, you will intersect Naked Ground Trail after 1.8 miles. Naked Ground Trail follows Little Santeetlah Creek northwest into the Slickrock Wilderness Area. This walk stops at Adamcamp Branch, but the trail continues for 2.8 more miles, ending at Haoe Lead Trail. By following Naked Ground Trail to its terminus, this 4.2-mile stroll could be turned into an all-day 10-mile hike.

*J*oyce Kilmer Memorial Forest is a 3,800-acre patch of virgin forest in the southeast corner of the Joyce Kilmer–Slickrock and Citico Creek wilderness areas. The wilderness areas straddle our state's border with Tennessee, but the memorial forest—one of the few remaining tracts of never-logged land in the southern Appalachian Mountains—is in North Carolina.

The highlight of this walk is, of course, the trees. Massive Canadian hemlocks with girths of 10 feet or more grow along Little Santeetlah Creek, and improbably straight yellow poplars tower 150 feet above the slopes. But there are also hickories and hollies and magnolias, and gigantic oaks and maples and birches. Because of their size and beauty, this slice of Appalachia was set aside in 1936 as a memorial to Joyce Kilmer, the author of "Trees."

It's easy to criticize that rhyming doggerel of our grammar-school years. "Trees" is simplistic and sappy, and even when it was first published in 1913, one critic called it "artlessly naive."

But it's been reprinted and recited countless times, and something about it clearly strikes a chord in many of us. Perhaps it's the first two lines:

I think that I shall never see
A poem lovely as a tree.

The trees along this trail may cause you to agree with Kilmer. And the power of poetry should not be underestimated. After all, it saved the trees.

When a New York chapter of the Veterans of Foreign Wars asked the government to establish a memorial to Kilmer, his most famous poem must have immediately come to mind: someone decided that the only proper monument would be a virgin stand of timber. The task of finding it fell to the United States Forest Service. It wasn't an easy job; by the 1930s, most of the land in the East had been logged. Only a series of accidents had saved the Little Santeetlah Creek watershed, and the ax was on the way. When the forest service bought the land in 1935, the lumber company that owned it was ready to log it. Since that purchase, not much has happened. A few trails have been built, a few buildings have been put up, and—appropriately—a copy of "Trees" has been tacked to the wall of the shelter near the trailhead.

From the shelter, Joyce Kilmer Memorial Trail leads to a bridge across Little Santeetlah Creek—a rambunctious mountain stream in late spring when I walked there—then climbs gently into a forest of poplars and hemlocks. These are huge trees, but unlike the redwoods of California, they don't form tightly packed single-species groves. They each stand alone, separated from one another by space and species, only one part of this biologically diverse forest. Though the giants get most of the attention, there are wildflowers and poison oak and saplings, small trees, ordinary trees, and vines. There are nurse logs and lightning-splintered crags; there are mushrooms and mosses. Mature hardwood coves such as this one harbor an incredible variety of plant life, a heterogeneity comparable to that of a rain forest.

Where the Kilmer and Poplar Cove loops join, there is a state-record hemlock 15 feet around and over 150 feet tall. There is also a plaque that explains why the V.F.W. wanted this memorial. It reads, in part,

> *Joyce Kilmer*
> *165th Infantry, Rainbow Division, soldier and*
> *poet, author of "Trees", born in New Brunswick,*
> *N.J., December 6, 1886, killed in action in France*
> *July 30, 1918*

Joyce Kilmer died at age thirty-one while fighting in World War I, and it's fitting that his plaque and this ancient tree stand side by side: both he and the hemlock came from ages far different from our own.

The tree sprouted during Elizabethan times, while Kilmer was born in the late Victorian age. Both were times of great passions, times of relative innocence when ideals were worth dying for.

In our cynical age, it is almost impossible to imagine a young man with a burgeoning literary career and a job with the *New York Times* volunteering as a private in the army; almost impossible to imagine him plotting his way out of a cushy "bullet-proof" job so he could get to the front lines; almost impossible to imagine him requesting a transfer to a job that would take him *beyond* the front lines into no man's land. But Joyce Kilmer did all of these things. And he died for doing them, killed by an enemy bullet near the village of Seringes.

Kilmer's life, like his poetry, seems anachronistic today, and except for one poem, he would almost certainly be forgotten. But "Trees" continues to live, a survivor like the great hemlock, and as long as it does, a part of Joyce Kilmer will be with us. And if the poem lacks critical merit, you can't help but respect the man who created it and be touched by this memorial to him.

Just beyond the plaque, Poplar Cove Trail winds farther up the mountain. The reason for the trail's name becomes obvious as you walk. Gigantic yellow poplars are scattered over this north-facing slope. I didn't measure any of them, but one guide lists the largest as having a circumference of nearly twenty feet.

Near the trail, there's also a state-record cucumber tree, a magnolia that produces fruit resembling a cucumber. Umbrella and Fraser magnolias are also common here. Many of them appear to sit on stilts, their roots spreading conically into the soil, suspending the trees in midair. These magnolias sprouted on the decaying trunks of fallen trees. For their roots to reach the ground, they had to grow around the dead tree, and after the log—called a nurse log—rotted away, a row of stilt trees remained to commemorate the carcass that nurtured them.

After rejoining the lower loop, the trail eases back down to Little Santeetlah Creek. Immediately across the creek, Naked Ground Trail splits off to the left. It rises into the Unicoi Mountains, running through the heart of what used to be the

Cherokee nation. One historian claims that Naked Ground Trail was once a Cherokee trading path, but nobody knows for sure. It is known that in 1813, representatives from Tennessee, Georgia, and the Cherokee nation got together to lay out a public road from the coast to the white settlements in eastern Tennessee. The western part of the road—now long gone—followed Cherokee trails, and it ran through the Unicoi Mountains, possibly along this route.

As I walked the gentle grade, it was easy to imagine the trail as a Cherokee path. The tall trees and tiny wildflowers growing along it must have looked about the same in the mid-eighteenth century, the peak of Cherokee power and prosperity.

Until the French and Indian War, the Cherokees spent their time hunting and fishing, growing corn, and waging small wars with their neighbors, the Creeks, the Chickasaws, and the Catawbas. They were a powerful, well-organized tribe, and they won enough battles to maintain their territory and occasionally expand it a little. They also skirmished with the English settlers to the east and held their own with them, too.

But during the war, the Cherokees sided with the French, and the English got serious about curbing their power. The English allied themselves with the Chickasaws and the Catawbas. In 1760 and 1761, they raided Cherokee towns along the Tuckasegee and Little Tennessee rivers, burning villages and the corn that was stored in them. The Cherokees were in bad shape when the other shoe fell. A smallpox epidemic broke out. By the time they surrendered, half of their warriors were dead.

Fifteen years later, another war broke out—the American Revolution. Impressed by the British in peace and concerned about their prowess in war, the Cherokees sided with them. It was a bad choice; the colonists were even better Indian fighters than the British—and more ruthless.

In 1776, white Americans raided the Cherokees. Thirty-six of their towns were burned, the corn destroyed, the livestock killed or run off or stolen. Later, Echota, the ancient capital of the Cherokee nation, was destroyed, and the South Carolina legislature offered a bounty of seventy-five pounds for Cherokee scalps.

Time and again the white men came, razing villages and burning fields. And when the war ended, smallpox again raged through the ragged survivors. The Cherokees were thoroughly defeated.

Somehow, they bounced back. They sided with the United States in the War of 1812; they helped Andrew Jackson defeat the Creeks in the battle of Horseshoe Bend; they became literate overnight after Sequoyah invented an alphabet; and they signed treaty after treaty with the United States, only to have them broken. Although they adapted to white ways faster than most Native Americans, it was a game they couldn't win. The whites were too strong, too treacherous, and though the Cherokees' numbers swelled again, their land was gradually sheared from them by treaty and by purchase.

The end began in 1828, when gold was discovered on Cherokee land in northern Georgia. For whites to get at it, the Cherokees had to go. Ten years later, they were "removed" to Oklahoma over a route now called the Trail of Tears. Four thousand of them died on the march.

A few eluded the soldiers and stayed. They became the nucleus of the eastern band of the Cherokee nation. Many of their descendants live on the Qualla Boundary Reservation to the east, but some live in towns and on farms near the Unicoi Mountains. Of course, no Cherokees (or anyone else) live in Joyce Kilmer now, but walking up Naked Ground Trail, I was able to imagine the ghosts of Cherokees trotting silently by, hurrying to Echota.

Farther up the trail, a bridge spans Adamcamp Branch. On the far side, moss-covered logs lie scattered in the forest. This is a graveyard, a reminder of how this country has changed. Though I imagined this to be the same forest that the Cherokees knew, it isn't. The chestnuts are gone.

The American chestnut, *Castanea dentata*, once grew over most of the eastern United States. Its wood was strong and rot resistant, its nuts delicious and filling. In *Walden*, Thoreau wrote, "When the chestnuts were ripe I laid up half a bushel for winter." A century ago, families in these mountains did the same. The nuts were easy to find in those days; over a quarter of the trees in parts of the southern Appalachian forest were chestnuts.

The chestnut blight came to these mountains from the Orient by way of New York. Around the turn of the century, Asiatic chestnuts carrying the blight were imported into the city. The Japanese and Chinese varieties of chestnut are blight resistant, but the American chestnut is not. The disease was first discovered in 1904 on chestnut trees at the Bronx Zoo. During the next fifty years, it killed virtually every American chestnut. "Chestnut blight is the most destructive plant disease known," said one plant pathologist in 1969.

What is this blight, this destroyer of chestnuts? It's a fungus, *Endothia parasitica*. Fungi obtain food by functioning as either

saprophytes or parasites. Saprophytic fungi feed on the dead. One example is the mushroom, sucking nourishment from rotting trees. But parasites feed on the living, and *Endothia parasitica*, as its name implies, is a parasitic fungus.

There are many parasitic fungi. They cause everything from clubroot in plants to athlete's foot in humans. They cause powdery mildew, rust, leaf-curl, and smut. Some, like *Endothia*, are almost impossible to control because they produce millions of microscopic spores, wind-borne poisons which spread quickly.

The blight reached the South in the 1920s, and by 1940 most of the chestnuts that once blanketed these mountains were dead. At Adamcamp Branch, I could see the result: chestnut corpses lying on the forest floor, their rot-resistant wood finally rotting away, testaments to the awesome efficiency of *Endothia*.

But no predator is perfect. Because the blight attacks only through the bark, the chestnuts' roots remain unaffected. Twenty years ago, even a casual eye could spot numerous stumps with sprouts growing from the roots. But the roots eventually die, and there are not as many sprouts today as there used to be. I looked carefully for them during my walk and found only one, a healthy, ten-foot-tall American chestnut. The blight will get it soon, but as long as even a few are around, there's hope.

In his 1979 book, *Tree Nuts*, J. G. Woodroof, a man who worked with trees for most of his life, said, "The prevailing opinion of foresters and pathologists is that the American chestnut will come back on its own by natural selection." I remembered Woodroof's statement as I rubbed my hand over the still-intact heartwood center of one of the decomposing logs at Adamcamp Branch, and I tried to carry his optimism back down the trail with me.

Mountain laurels were shedding their flowers, and the fallen petals brightened the forest floor. Wildflowers flourished along the sides of the trail. Although few were blooming at that time of year, I identified galax and trillium and columbine. There were lilies and ferns of all sorts and more Indian pipes than I'd ever seen. Rhododendron blossoms were ready to burst, and I saw one flashy but lonely flame azalea, bright orange against the green.

These are much-traveled trails, and I saw little wildlife on my walk. Birds called to one another and rustled in the understory, but the only creature I could identify for sure was a snake I almost stepped on. It slithered off the trail where it had been taking the sun and paused long enough for me to get a good look. It was a brown snake, a small slug-eating snake of the moist uplands. Its skin was so dry- and smooth-looking that I reached down to touch its tail, but it avoided my hand and slid into a pile of rocks and vanished.

In late spring, the mountain nights are cool, and snakes find the patches of morning sunlight irresistible. As I was leaving Joyce Kilmer, I spotted a large black snake coiled on the centerline of the highway. It looked like a black racer, a graceful, fast-moving snake, but from the car, it was hard to be sure. As I watched in my rearview mirror, the car behind me swerved and ran over it. The snake, still coiled, was thrown high into the air. When it came down, it didn't move.

I pulled over to let the car pass; I wanted to see what kind of person would go out of his way to kill a snake sunning itself on the road. I hoped to see a black hat or a tattoo that read "Villain" or some other identifying mark that would separate him from the rest of us. But all I saw was an ordinary-looking man driving an ordinary-looking car.

It would be nice to think that ordinary men didn't do such things in Joyce Kilmer's idealistic age, but they did. And if modern attitudes are more cynical about war, they're considerably more generous toward wildlife. It's just that some people—like the driver of that car—are slow to catch the new drift. It'll come, though. All we need is the right poet.

Before You Go

For More Information ———————————————————
United States Forest Service
Cheoah Ranger District
Route 1, Box 16-A
Robbinsville, N.C. 28771
(704) 479-6431

Accommodations

The closest town to Joyce Kilmer is Robbinsville. For information, call or write

Graham County Travel and Tourism Authority
P.O. Box 1206
Robbinsville, N.C. 28771
(704) 479-3790

Snowbird Mountain Lodge
275 Santeetlah Road
Robbinsville, N.C. 28771
(704) 479-3433

Another possibility is Bryson City. It's farther from Joyce Kilmer, but the town has a nice selection of motels, inns, and lodges. For information, contact

Swain County Chamber of Commerce
P.O. Box 509
Bryson City, N.C. 28713
(704) 488-3681

Campgrounds

Horse Cove Campground lies on Santeetlah Creek near the entrance to Joyce Kilmer. Its seventeen campsites are administered by the Cheoah Ranger District of Nantahala National Forest.

Maps

A topographic map of the Joyce Kilmer–Slickrock and Citico Creek wilderness areas can be bought at the Cheoah District Office on Massey Branch Road, 2 miles northwest of Robbinsville. But the map in Tim Homan's book (see the "Additional Reading" section) is all you'll need, and it's more accurate to boot.

Points of Interest _____

Dave Gustafson, a ranger at the Cheoah District Office, said that the trail to Hangover—a rocky outcrop north of Little Santeetlah Creek—offers a fine walk with excellent views. The walk starts at Wolf Laurel Trail.

Additional Reading

Fungal Parasitism by Brian J. Deverall, St. Martin's Press, New York, 1969.

Hiking Trails of Joyce Kilmer–Slickrock and Citico Creek Wilderness Areas by Tim Homan, Peachtree Publishers, Atlanta, 1990.

Historical Sketch of the Cherokee by James Mooney, Smithsonian Institution Press, Washington, D.C., 1975.

I Lay Down My Life: Biography of Joyce Kilmer by Harry J. Cargas, St. Paul Editions, Boston, 1964.

Joyce Kilmer edited with a memoir by Robert Cortes Halliday, George H. Doran Company, New York, 1914.

Trail of Tears: The Rise and Fall of the Cherokee Nation by John Ehle, Anchor Books/Doubleday, New York, 1988.

Tree Nuts by J. G. Woodroof, AVI Publishing Company, Westport, Conn., 1979.

Trees by Joyce Kilmer, George H. Doran Company, New York, 1914.

Eno River State Park

THE PIEDMONT

In the mean time, we went to shoot Pigeons, which were so numerous in these Parts, that you might see many Millions in a Flock; they sometimes split off the limbs of stout Oaks and other Trees, upon which they roost o' Nights.

John Lawson, 1709

Length: 7 miles

**Degree
of Difficulty: Easy to Moderate**

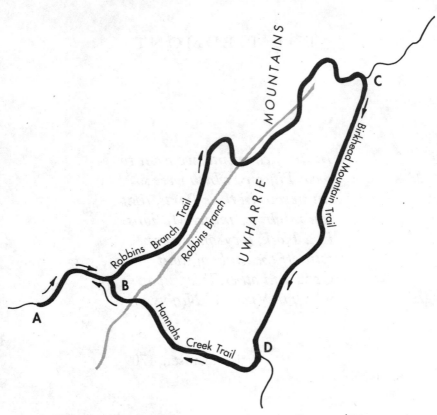

Birkhead Mountains Wilderness

A. Parking lot for Birkhead
   Mountains Wilderness
B. Junction Robbins Branch Trail
   and Hannahs Creek Trail
C. Junction Robbins Branch Trail
   and Birkhead Mountain Trail
D. Junction Birkhead Mountain Trail
   and Hannahs Creek Trail

Route and Distances

A. to B.	0.4 mi.
B. to C.	2.8 mi.
C. to D.	2.0 mi.
D. to B.	1.4 mi.
B. to A.	0.4 mi.
TOTAL	7.0 mi.

The Oldest Hills

Robbins Branch–Birkhead Mountain–Hannahs Creek Loop
Birkhead Mountains Wilderness
Uwharrie National Forest

From Asheboro, take N.C. 49 west for 5 miles to Mechanic Road, then go south on it to an intersection with State Road 1107 (Lassiter Mill Road). Continue south on Lassiter Mill Road for 3 miles, then go left on Forest Road 6532 (a rough dirt road) and proceed east for 0.5 mile to the parking lot for Birkhead Mountains Wilderness. Robbins Branch Trail begins there. Walk north, then east on Robbins Branch Trail for 0.4 mile to a junction with Hannahs Creek Trail. Stay left on Robbins Branch Trail and proceed north, roughly paralleling Robbins Branch. Near the stream's source, the trail turns east and climbs to intersect Birkhead Mountain Trail 3.2 miles from the trailhead. Proceed south on Birkhead Mountain Trail for 2 miles to its intersection with Hannahs Creek Trail. Take Hannahs Creek Trail east for 1.4 miles to Robbins Branch Trail. From there, it is 0.4 mile back to the trailhead.

*The region, known as the Uwharrie Mountains,
has been mistakenly described as the "oldest
mountains in North America." While the rocks of the
Uwharries are Precambrian in age [at least 550
million years old], the erosion that created today's
land surface is very young in geologic terms.*

Fred Beyer

he Birkhead Mountains are part of the Uwharries, a range of stubby mountains that lies well east of the Appalachians, in an area where there should be no mountains. Articles about the Uwharries that appear in newspapers and magazines often claim that they are the oldest mountains in North

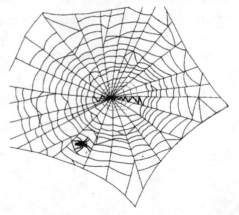

America. This is not a claim supported by many geologists. Al Carpenter, senior geologist with the North Carolina Geological Survey, says that rocks found in the Appalachians are as old as, or older than, those found in the Uwharries. He adds in a bemused tone that he has no idea how such a story got started. But it's an engaging story, and it suggests a question: how old *are* the Uwharries? The complex geologic history of the region precludes a simple answer, but it is a question worth exploring before setting foot in these hills.

As mountains erode, rainfall washes weathered fragments away, and streams and rivers deposit them at lower altitudes. This leveling creates a peneplain—a landscape of rolling hills not quite flat enough to be called a plain—that slopes gently down to the sea. Over millions of years, this flake-by-flake movement of mountains toward the sea shifts the weight on the crustal plate, which floats on a mantle of plastic rock that surrounds the earth's core. The redistribution of weight on the plate's surface causes it to tilt, raising the land on one side, lowering it on the other.

Twenty million years ago, North Carolina and much of the eastern United States was covered by the Schooley peneplain. As the peneplain formed, the eastern edge of the continental plate tilted downward and thrust the Appalachians high into the air, creating the eastern continental divide. As the rivers coursed eastward out of the mountains, hard rock was eaten away more slowly than softer rock, causing the Schooley peneplain to erode unevenly. The hard erosional remnants—the tops of which were once part of the surface of the old Schooley peneplain—are called monadnocks, and they are found today all through the Appalachians and the Piedmont. One group of these monadnocks is called the Uwharrie Mountains, and the Birkhead Mountains are the northernmost range in that group.

They were named for John Watson Birkhead, a farmer who acquired 3,000 acres of those rolling hills near the end of the nineteenth century. Although he moved to Asheboro in 1914 after his house on the property burned, he continued to farm the land until 1933. Soon afterward, the federal government acquired the property of Birkhead and others in the vicinity as part of a nationwide program to help Depression-wracked farmers and convert submarginal farmland back to forests. Collectively, the lands bought from Birkhead and his neighbors were called the Uwharrie Purchase Unit. In 1961, the purchase unit's 43,000 acres were designated as the Uwharrie National Forest, and in 1984, nearly 5,000 acres of this forest were set aside as the Birkhead Mountains Wilderness.

By all accounts, the properties in the Uwharrie Purchase Unit were overlogged and farmed-out when the government bought them. But the years since have been better to the land, especially to the Birkheads. The slopes and ridges of the range have reseeded naturally, and the result is a fine oak-hickory forest, the climax forest of much of the outer Piedmont—the portion of the Piedmont farthest from the Appalachians.

It is a forest that is especially attractive in the fall, when the yellows of the hickories and the brownish reds of the oaks contrast with one another in the canopy, and when fallen leaves of every shade soften the forest floor. So I choose the end of October for a walk in the Birkheads.

I start on Robbins Branch Trail on a cool, bright day. Sizable rocks gleam from the slopes. Quartzite found north of here in the Sauratown Mountains has been identified as being the metamorphosed remains of the sandy bottom of the Iapatos Ocean—an ocean that covered the region 800 million years ago. Although no similar quartzite has been found in the Uwharries, this land, too, once lay at the bottom of that ocean, and the shining rocks remind me of how far back these mountains' geologic history can be traced.

The most striking feature of the trail, however, is not the rocks but the variety of small trees that grow near the path. In the first quarter of a mile, I pass red oaks and red maples, hickories, white oaks, blackjack oaks and small cedars, beeches, and rust-red dogwoods. Sweet gums cling to leaves made purple by autumn, and dry, brown oak leaves crackle beneath my feet.

Deeper in the forest, beyond the intersection with Hannahs Creek Trail, post oaks, chestnut oaks, and tulip poplars become more common. Chickadees call from the trees, and turkey vultures circle overhead. Orb weavers have been at work during the night, and brown-and-red and yellow-and-black spiders scurry to safety up filaments of silver as I crash through web after web spun invisibly across the trail. The contours of the hills are gentle, so the ups and downs of the path are mild and the walking is pleasant.

Near the top of a ridge, a huge white oak that must have been spared by generations of axmen shades an understory of bright red sourwoods and dark green Christmas ferns. The cries of the chickadees intensify. I glimpse a speck of white and a flit of gray in the branches of the oak.

Two species of chickadees live in North Carolina, the black-capped (*Parus atricapillus*) and the Carolina (*Parus carolinensis*). The Carolina chickadee is about an inch shorter than the black-capped version, and its song is said to be higher pitched. Otherwise, the two species are identical, and unless you have unusually well-calibrated eyes and ears, the only way to tell them apart in North Carolina is by their location. And in winter, even that method won't work.

Black-capped chickadees are birds of the North; the mountains of North Carolina are about as far south as they range. The black-capped chickadees that do live here summer in the Great Smokies and other mountains, usually at altitudes greater than four thousand feet. But in the colder months, they drift down to lower elevations and mingle with Carolina chickadees, making winter birders guess at which species they are watching. Since there has not been a cold spell yet this year, I assume these birds are Carolina chickadees.

But it makes little difference; both species are twitchy little packages of nervous energy. Though they are easy to find anywhere in the state, their quick movements make them hard to study in the forest. The best place to observe chickadees is at a bird feeder at home. You won't have any trouble attracting them; they adore sunflower seeds. But unlike finches and doves, which will sit on a feeder for minutes at a time methodically munching down seed, chickadees do it the hard way, one seed per trip.

I've always enjoyed watching them. They fly to the feeder, look around defiantly, grab a seed, then streak back to a branch in a nearby tree. There, they look around again, spread their tiny, pipestem legs, and start hammering the seed on the branch between their feet until they break open the shell. Then they extract the kernel, swallow it, and it's back to the feeder for another seed.

In the Carolina woods, where there are no bird feeders or sunflower seeds, much of their diet is made up of caterpillars and spiders and beetles. I've never seen chickadees feeding in the forest, so I have no idea how they handle their catch. But I can imagine it; I can almost see one of them up there in the oak, beetle clasped firmly in its beak, looking around, then whacking that poor bug on a twig until it's pulpy enough for lunch.

Beyond the oak, the trail continues to parallel Robbins Branch, leaf clogged, shallow, and barely flowing in this dry season. Big four-winged creatures flush from the ground in front of me and fly noisily into the tops of trees. I never get close enough to unequivocally identify one, but they flush like quail and are almost as large as hummingbirds, so my guess is they are American bird grasshoppers—an aptly named insect if ever there was one.

After a mile or so, the creek disappears, and the trail turns east and begins to climb. At the intersection with Birkhead Mountain Trail, I turn south and follow it along a ridge. Tightly packed groves of red-maple and oak saplings no bigger around than a half dollar cover the slopes, but the trail soon enters an older forest of larger trees. Tulip poplars, their leaves the color of perfect toast at this time of year, are the tallest of them, and the bright yellow hickories are the most colorful, but the white oaks with their huge, spreading canopies are surely the most impressive flora in the oak-hickory forest.

White oak (*Quercus alba*) is a common and valuable tree of the eastern United States—and has been for some time. From southern Maine to northern Florida, white oak was the early settlers' choice for many of their everyday needs; its timber built the ships and barns and bridges of our young country. Today, it goes into fireplaces and furniture and floors. In North Carolina, which has fifteen species of oaks scattered throughout the state, white oak is found mainly in the Piedmont. Black oak also does well here. These two species are the principal large oaks of Piedmont forests.

Q. alba is a slow-growing, long-lived oak, and logging has reduced the number of mature trees. The three-hundred-year-old giants that were common in the Piedmont's virgin forests are rare today. Some of the white oaks in the Birkheads are eight or nine feet around and perhaps a hundred years old. But a one-hundred-year-old white oak still has a lot of growing to do. The largest white oak standing today is a hundred-foot-tall gem in Wye Mills, Maryland. Its trunk is almost thirty feet around, and its canopy is broad enough to shade half a football field at high noon.

Beneath the tulip trees and oaks, a healthy understory of maples, cedars, and hollies flourishes. A rich shrub layer of blueberries and huckleberries grows below them. Still lower to the ground is the herbaceous layer—which along this trail consists primarily of Christmas ferns. But occasionally, unusual streaks of bright green zigzag through this lowest layer of plants. The green streaks are running cedar (*Lycopodium clavatum*), a plant that is collected and sold to florists for Christmas garlands. It is a misnamed plant, not a cedar at all. Rather, it is a club moss, one of the more primitive plants in the world and a relative of the first living things to inch out of the sea and establish themselves on dry land.

At the intersection of Birkhead Mountain and Hannahs Creek trails, a sign says that Christopher Bingham's plantation, built about 1780, once stood here. And though I see nothing to suggest that humans ever occupied this patch of land, the sign is a reminder that the history of the Uwharries is not just one of ancient peneplains and plants. The Uwharries have a human history as well, one that began long before the Binghams built their plantation.

Archaeologists have discovered that extensive quarrying took place in the southern Uwharries as long as 11,000 years ago. Much as white Americans were drawn to these mountains by the discovery of gold in the early nineteenth century, Native Americans flocked to the Uwharries for Morrow Mountain rhyolite, a volcanic rock similar to obsidian—and far more important to them than gold. Hard yet easy to cleave, rhyolite was ideal for the cutting and hunting implements of the earliest Americans. The properties that made it so valuable developed at the time the rocks were formed, a time long before the Schooley peneplain.

Basalt and granite are two types of igneous rock. Both are formed when molten rock, or magma, rises from the earth's mantle. As it nears the surface, it cools and solidifies. Magma that cools slowly underground forms coarse-grained, crystalline rocks, but if it reaches the surface of the earth in molten form (where it is called lava), it solidifies quickly, forming fine-grained rocks. Most lava is basaltic and produces the dense—almost glassy—black rocks that can be seen at the base of most active volcanoes. But some lava is granitic, and when it cools, the result is a hard, fine-grained rock known as rhyolite. The volcanoes which erupted here 500 million years ago spewed out granitic lava, and though erosion has worn the volcanoes themselves away, the rhyolite they produced is still around. And its fine-grained texture allowed the first inhabitants of these hills to knap it easily into the extremely hard hand axes and spear points they so prized.

The last leg of the walk parallels Hannahs Creek. Wealth seekers once panned this creek for another geological rarity—gold. From 1802 until well into the twentieth century, men and women came to the Uwharries to strike it rich. Mines were located along the Uwharrie River and its tributaries. How well the gold hunters did at Hannahs Creek was not recorded, but the stream is a bare trickle today, and in this season, it would take a very patient panner indeed to glean a living from it.

Gold is present in all igneous rock, though its concentration is usually too low to make its extraction profitable. Geologists are not sure of the origin of the gold-enriched veins and nuggets that touched off the Carolina gold rush. One theory says that high concentrations of gold are dissolved in some of the molten rock that wells up from deep inside the earth. If so, the source of Uwharrie gold might have been the same ancient magma that became the rhyolite so valued by Indians. Or it might have risen from the depths in an even more ancient upheaval, surfacing only recently as streams and weather eroded the hills down to even older rock.

So how old *are* the Uwharries? How old is man? We humans—like white oaks, chickadees, and running cedar—trace our lineage back 3.5 billion years to the first cell. Since then, the life and death of every living creature has affected the path of evolution and, therefore, of humans as well. Mountains, like men, are formed by processes that begin at birth. And though approximate dates can be assigned to each stage in the evolution of the Uwharries—from the sandy beaches laid down by the ancient Iapatos Ocean, to the rhyolite-producing volcanoes, to the uneven erosion of the Schooley peneplain—no single date completely answers the question. How old are these mountains? Pick the date that suits you; to me, they are as old as the earth itself.

Before You Go

For More Information ⸻
Uwharrie National Forest
Route 3, Box 470
Troy, N.C. 27371
(919) 576-6391

Accommodations ⸻
Asheboro/Randolph Chamber of Commerce
317 East Dixie Drive
Asheboro, N.C. 27203

(919) 626-2626

Campgrounds

The United States Forest Service maintains a large tent and trailer campground at Badin Lake. There are two more campgrounds at Morrow Mountain State Park, just west of the Uwharrie National Forest.

Primitive camping is permitted anywhere in the back country of the national forest and in the Birkhead Mountains Wilderness.

Maps

A trail map for the Birkhead Mountains Wilderness is available for $2 from the United States Forest Service. The forest service also sells a map of the entire Uwharrie National Forest for the same price. Although this map is not detailed enough to serve as a guide to the Birkhead trails, it will help you find the trailhead, a not-to-be-taken-for-granted task in an area that is as crisscrossed with bumpy forest roads as this one.

Points of Interest

Morrow Mountain State Park lies southwest of the Birkhead Mountains on the western side of the Pee Dee River. The 4,693-acre park has over 30 miles of hiking and bridle trails and is capped by 936-foot-tall Morrow Mountain, the highest peak in the park. For more information, contact

Morrow Mountain State Park
Route 5, Box 430
Albemarle, N.C. 28001
(704) 982-4402

A few miles south of the Uwharries, archaeologists have partially excavated an Indian village at Town Creek Indian Mound State Historic Site. A visitor center exhibits artifacts from the village, and a slide show tells something of the culture of the Native Americans of the region. For information, contact

Town Creek Indian Mound
Route 3, Box 50
Mount Gilead, N.C. 27306

Additional Reading

The Audubon Society Encyclopedia of North American Birds by John K. Terres, Wings Press, New York, 1991. This book was originally published by Alfred A. Knopf and was last copyrighted by them in 1980.

Birds of the Carolinas by Eloise F. Potter, James F. Parnell, and Robert P. Teulings, University of North Carolina Press, Chapel Hill, 1980.

Common Forest Trees of North Carolina, 15th ed., originally prepared by J. S. Holmes, North Carolina Department of Natural Resources, Division of Forest Products, Raleigh, 1983.

"The Establishment of the Uwharrie National Forest: National Policies and Local Contexts" by Martin Nash, master's thesis, University of North Carolina at Charlotte, 1980.

Extinction: Bad Genes or Bad Luck? by David M. Raup, W. W. Norton and Company, New York, 1991.

The Forging of Our Continent by Charlton Ogburn, Jr., American Heritage Publishing Company, New York, 1968.

"Inselbergs on the Piedmont of Virginia, North Carolina, and South Carolina: Types and Characteristics" by Richard H.

Kesel, *Southeastern Geology* 16, 1974, 1–30.

The Klamath Knot by David Rains Wallace, Sierra Club Books, San Francisco, 1983.

A Natural History of Trees of Eastern and Central North America by Donald Culross Peattie, Houghton Mifflin Company, Boston, 1948.

North Carolina: The Years Before Man by Fred Beyer, Carolina Academic Press, Durham, N.C., 1991.

The Practical Botanist by Rick Imes, Simon and Schuster, New York, 1990.

"Rambling the Uwharries" by Jane Rohling, *Wildlife in North Carolina* 48, August 1984, 16–22.

A Sierra Club Naturalist's Guide to the Piedmont by Michael A. Godfrey, Sierra Club Books, San Francisco, 1980.

Length: 4.9 miles

**Degree
of Difficulty: Easy**

Eno River

Cox Mountain Trail

E

D

Fanny's Ford Trail

Wilderness
Shelter
Access Trail

C

Swinging Footbridge

Eno River

B

A

Eno Trace
Nature Trail

Parking
Lot

Cole Mill Road

Eno River Trails

A. Start here
B. Eno Trace Nature Trail
C. Begin Cox Mountain Loop
D. Begin Fanny's Ford Loop
E. Begin path back to trailhead

Route and Distances

A. to B. to A.	0.4 mi.
A. to C.	0.7 mi.
C. to D.	2.1 mi.
D. to E.	0.9 mi.
E. to A.	0.8 mi.
TOTAL	4.9 mi.

A Walk along a River

Eno Trace Nature Trail-Cox Mountain Trail
Fanny's Ford Trail
Eno River State Park

From I-85, exit onto Cole Mill Road. Follow
Cole Mill Road north until it dead-ends at
Few's Ford Access. The trails start from the
back parking lot. This walk begins with the Eno
Trace Nature Trail. Its twelve interpretive posts
will acquaint you with some of the flora and
fauna of the Piedmont. After finishing the
nature trail, cross the Eno River on the
swinging footbridge and continue north 0.7
mile on Wilderness Shelter Access Trail to Cox
Mountain Trail. Near the end of the Cox
Mountain loop, go left on Fanny's Ford Trail.
Follow it clockwise back to Wilderness Shelter
Access Trail and return south on the access trail
to the parking lot.

*D*urham has changed. When we used to go there years ago, we thought Turnages was the best restaurant in town. It was an all-you-can-eat Durham institution filled with rows of oilcloth-covered picnic tables. On each table were a loaf of white bread, a pot of Brunswick stew, two pitchers of sweetened iced tea, and a great, worn wooden bowl which was kept filled by grandmotherly waitresses with the finest chopped barbecue in the South. For grad students like us, forever on the edge of poverty and always hungry, Saturday night at Turnages was a time to seriously stoke up.

In Durham these days, all-

you-can-eat barbecue joints have gone the way of passenger pigeons. In their place are upscale restaurants with chalkboards out front that advertise gazpacho, pasta salads, alfalfa-sprout sandwiches, and the wine of the day. Places where water comes in bottles and costs more than iced tea. But even as the town remakes itself to join the new urban South, one Durham institution remains unchanged: its river. The Eno flows through the town's suburbs just north of the city limits, but Durhamites consider it *their* river. And over the years, they have taken good care of it; the Eno is still a fine place for a walk. In fact, it's even better than it used to be. Now, there's a park along its banks.

The 2,064-acre Eno River State Park lies west of Durham. It is divided into four sections, each offering access to the river. The longest walk is in the Few's Ford section. Three trails—the short Eno Trace Nature Trail, Cox Mountain Trail, and Fanny's Ford Trail—start near the swinging bridge that spans the river at Few's Ford. When combined, they form a loop that is part river stroll, part walk in the woods, and entirely pleasant.

Like most of the Piedmont, the park is far from being a primeval wilderness; the last stand of virgin forest was cut in 1941. Today, the land is covered by forests in transition, with the early-growth pines and cedars gradually being succeeded by the hardwoods of the climax forest.

Although forests in various stages of succession are clearly visible on this walk, the first thing you notice is the river. You hear it before you see it. Then, as you descend a bluff on the nature trail, it comes into view, sliding around a bend, running clear in a rocky bed, looking more like a big mountain stream than a sluggish river of the Piedmont. In 1979, while putting together the park's master plan, hydrologists studied the Eno.

They found it to be a clean river; in some sections, the water was classified as drinkable without any purification. Today, even though park officials strongly advise against drinking the water, the Eno is still one of the cleanest rivers in the state.

On this walk, the old is jammed against the new. There are power lines and fence posts, old fields and mill ruins. And then there is the river, sparkling and bright, essentially unchanged from the day John Lawson, who would later become surveyor-general of North Carolina, traveled through these parts. That was in 1701, and his guide and host was an Indian named Enoe-Will.

In her history of Durham County, Jean Anderson quotes from Lawson's account of his visit to an Indian village on the Eno River. The Enos rolled out the red carpet, feeding Lawson and his party "fat Bear" and "barbekued . . . Venison"—the earliest mention I've ever seen of barbecue in America. Enoe-Will—probably the chief of the tribe—stopped by their camp to make sure they were well fed.

The following morning, Enoe-Will accompanied the party to its next destination. Later, Lawson characterized his guide as "being always ready to serve the *English*, not out of Gain, but real Affection."

Historians believe that Enoe-Will reappears as "Shacco Will" in William Byrd's *Journey to the Land of Eden*. He was an old man by then, trying to sell Byrd a silver mine on the Eno River. Byrd didn't buy the mine but slipped him a bottle of rum, and Enoe-Will, fulfilling his final duty as a metaphor for his tribe, vanished from history.

What happened to the Eno Indians? Nobody knows for sure, but by the mid-eighteenth century they were gone. Some of

them probably migrated, joining stronger tribes to the north and south. But mostly—like the barbecue shacks of the fifties—the Enos just seemed to vanish, and since they went quietly, hardly anybody noticed. It was a vigorous age, and there was a country to build.

Settlers poured into the region. Over thirty gristmills sprouted along the Eno, raised by the English and Scotch-Irish farmers that immigrated to the state. Even today, the road that parallels the Eno retains a commercial air, with golf courses and shops and restaurants mixed with churches and housing developments. Although ruins of these old mills can be found within the park, you have to take a short trip downstream to West Point on the Eno to see what one looked like in the eighteenth century. The city of Durham has reconstructed a gristmill there, one originally built in 1778.

The park itself has a pleasant suburban atmosphere, more like that of a big backyard than a state park. But the relationship between the town of Durham and this land has not always been so cozy. In fact, the impetus to create the park started with a proposal by the Durham Department of Water Resources in 1966. The department wanted to dam the free-flowing Eno to create a reservoir that would have flooded the land where the park now sits.

Margaret Nygard, a landowner near the Eno, worked to save the river and her land. She formed the Association for the Preservation of the Eno River Valley. She talked and fought and organized. She got help from the Nature Conservancy, and after a tough three-year fight, her coalition finally prevailed. According to Nygard, the "regional planners rearranged their priorities" in 1969, and the Eno was moved to the bottom of their list as a possible reservoir site.

But the association was not finished. In 1970, its members presented a plan for a park to the North Carolina State Parks Division. The response was enthusiastic. Land was acquired, and Eno River State Park was created in 1973.

I knew some of this history when I started my walk, but by the time I finished the nature trail and began the pleasant climb up the wide path to Cox Mountain, I had managed to forget most of it. The simple, rhythmic act of walking worked its usual magic, and for the moment, the hard work that had gone into creating the park became less important than simply enjoying it.

The mild, rolling hills of the Piedmont produce the quintessential Southern forest, the forest that comes to mind when you think of the South. On the day of my walk, the dogwoods were in bloom, and their off-white flowers stood out against the new green of early spring. There were oaks and loblolly pines and wild azaleas. Wildflowers that looked like tiny white windmills were growing along the path, and the music of many birds filled the soft air. I recognized a few of the voices, but one of them persisted throughout my walk. It was loud, insistent, and ever-varying. Mockingbirds, those most Southern of birds, were everywhere.

The mockingbird's scientific name is *Mimus polyglottos*, or "many-tongued mimic," and, as usual, the Latin name is right on the money. Mockingbirds can imitate almost anything, and they remember what they've imitated. Every male mockingbird has its own repertoire, which it will run through at the slightest excuse—over and over again. In *Pilgrim at Tinker Creek*, Annie Dillard talks about a mockingbird serenading the opposite sex from the top of her chimney. "He sings a phrase and repeats it

exactly; then he sings another and repeats that, then another. . . .
He is tireless, too," she adds a trifle wearily. "Toward June he
will begin his daily marathon at two in the morning and scarcely
pause for breath until eleven at night. I don't know when he
sleeps."

Along these trails, the works of man are almost as evident as
mockingbirds. Stubby red cedars and scrawny young pines are
colonizing fields that were farmland until recently, and dilapidated fences still outline the borders of old meadows. But as I
came down from the hills and walked toward the river, I noticed
our forebears' footprints getting lighter. This is the river that
Enoe-Will knew. Large sycamores and sweet gums still grow
along its banks, bass and bluegill still swim in its pools, and
beavers still dam the creeks that feed it.

I didn't see any beavers during my walk, but their signatures
were everywhere. By the time I reached Fanny's Ford Trail—
the last leg of the hike—I had passed many gnawed stumps that
resembled the stubs of crudely sharpened pencils, along with a
number of girdled trees with the bottom two or three feet of
bark stripped away. But though their habits are the same, these
beavers did not descend from the ones that dammed the river in
Enoe-Will's day. These are imports.

In *Wildlife in America*, Peter Matthiessen traces the beginning of the beavers' decline to 1638, when King Charles
mandated the use of their pelts in the manufacture of hats. By
the time the hats went out of style, the beavers of North
America had been decimated. Only a few survived anywhere in
the East, and the largest rodent in North America was gone
completely from North Carolina.

In the 1920s, beavers from Wisconsin were reintroduced into

Pennsylvania. They did so well that some of them were livetrapped and released in North Carolina. The beavers of the Eno probably came from this stock. They're Midwesterners with a Yankee accent.

Their well-traveled history may account for their adaptability. After decades of watching floods sweep away their lodges, these beavers—unlike their stubborn Southern predecessors—gave up trying to dam the Eno a few years back and now live in burrows under its banks.

But sometimes stubbornness pays off. Margaret Nygard was stubborn, and because of her, the rest of us have a park. When I asked her what she remembered most about her long struggle, she said, "Nobody believed we could do it. *Nobody* thought that dam could be stopped."

Nygard spoke with a faint accent. It turned out she's British—like the early settlers along the river. And I guess our stubbornness came from them, so their legacy is almost as important to us Southerners as Enoe-Will's. But not quite. As best I can tell, he invented barbecue.

Before You Go

For More Information _____
Eno River State Park
Route 2, Box 436-C
Durham, N.C. 27687
(919) 383-1686

Accommodations _____
Durham Visitors Center
P.O. Box 3536
Durham, N.C. 27702
(800) 448-8604

Campgrounds _____
   Twenty-five primitive campsites are available to groups and families
at Few's Ford Access. The sites are about 1 mile from the parking
area. All supplies, including water, must be packed into the campground
and all garbage packed out.

Maps _____
   The trails are well marked, and the map in the park's free brochure
is adequate for this walk.

Points of Interest _____
   West Point on the Eno, a restored gristmill, is typical of the mills
that once lined the Eno River. A signed exit on I-85 a few miles east
of the Cole Mill Road exit leads to the mill.

Additional Reading

Durham County by Jean Bradley Anderson, Duke University
Press, Durham, N.C., 1990.

Eno River Master Plan by the State of North Carolina
Department of Natural Resources and Community
Development, Division of Parks and Recreation, Raleigh, June
1979.

"The Eno River of North Carolina" by Margaret Nygard,
Nature Conservancy News 23, Fall 1973, 10–15.

A New Voyage to Carolina by John Lawson, edited with an introduction and notes by Hugh Talmage Lefler, University of North Carolina Press, Chapel Hill, 1967. This book was first published in London in 1709.

Pilgrim at Tinker Creek by Annie Dillard, Harper's Magazine Press, New York, 1974.

A Sierra Club Naturalist's Guide to the Piedmont by Michael A. Godfrey, Sierra Club Books, San Francisco, 1980.

Wildlife in America by Peter Matthiessen, Viking Penguin, New York, 1987.

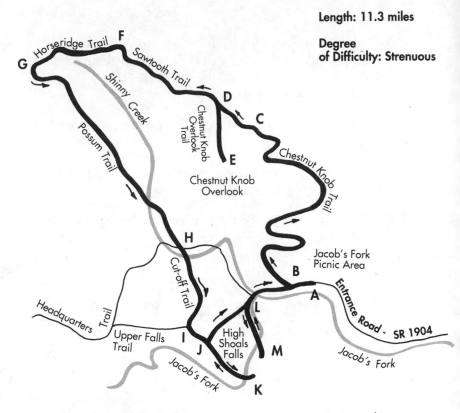

Length: 11.3 miles

**Degree
of Difficulty: Strenuous**

South Mountains State Park Route

A. Parking lot at Ranger Station
B. Junction Headquarters Trail
    and Chestnut Knob Trail
C. Junction Chestnut Knob Trail
    and Sawtooth Trail
D. Junction Sawtooth Trail and Chestnut
    Knob Overlook Trail
E. Chestnut Knob Overlook
F. Junction Sawtooth Trail and
    Horseridge Trail
G. Junction Horseridge Trail and Possum Trail
H. Junction Possum Trail and Cut-off Trail
I. Junction Cut-off Trail and Upper Falls Trail
J. Junction Cut-off Trail and unnamed trail
K. Upper Falls Overlook (top of falls)
L. Junction unnamed trail and High Shoals
    Falls Trail
M. High Shoals Falls Overlook (bottom of falls)

Route and Distances

A. to B.	0.1 mi.
B. to C.	2.0 mi.
C. to D.	0.2 mi.
D. to E.	0.3 mi.
E. to D.	0.3 mi.
D. to F.	0.8 mi.
F. to G.	0.8 mi.
G. to H.	2.2 mi.
H. to I.	0.8 mi.
I. to K.	0.6 mi.
K. to J.	0.4 mi.
J. to L.	0.5 mi.
L. to M.	0.9 mi.
M. to L.	0.9 mi.
M. to A.	0.5 mi.
TOTAL	**11.3 mi.**

The Mountains of the Piedmont

Chestnut Knob–High Shoals Falls Loop
South Mountains State Park

South Mountains State Park is located in Burke County 18 miles south of Morganton. From the Jacob's Fork picnic area and parking lot, Headquarters Trail, an old logging road, runs west into the interior of the park. At 0.1 mile, Chestnut Knob Trail leads north for 2 miles to Sawtooth Trail. Proceed west to Chestnut Knob Overlook Trail, then south to the overlook. Backtrack to Sawtooth Trail, continue northwest on it to Horseridge Trail, and take Horseridge Trail to Possum Trail. From that point, it is 2.2 miles to Cut-off Trail, a steep, uphill path that intersects with Upper Falls Trail. Follow Upper Falls Trail southeast to the top of High Shoals Falls. From the upper falls, retrace your footsteps for 0.4 mile to a Jeep road that leads northeast to Shinny Creek. Follow it to a signed trail that climbs to the lower falls. From the sign, the lower falls are a 1.8-mile round trip. The trailhead is 0.5 mile east by way of Headquarters Trail.

The great scarp of the Blue Ridge traces an arc across western North Carolina from Georgia to Virginia. Paralleling that arc, and about twenty miles east of it, is another, more irregular line of mountains. These mountains are not part of the Blue Ridge, and though they appear contiguous on a map, they do not form a ridge. Geologists call groups of these small, stand-alone mountain ranges plutons, and the South Mountains of southern Burke County are part of the Dysartsville pluton.

The mountains of this pluton are not as tall as the more famous peaks to the north and west. Mount Mitchell, only thirty-five miles west of the South Mountains, is over twice as tall as Buzzard Roost, which at 3,110 feet is the highest mountain in the range. Even so, like some of the other plutonic ranges in the otherwise gently rolling Piedmont, the South Mountains are steep and rocky, irregularly eroded by wind, weather, streams, and waterfalls, a terrain almost as rugged as the Blue Ridge itself—and far less visited.

They've always been that way—remote, isolated, and nearly deserted. Even the expansion-minded Cherokees never established permanent villages in the South Mountains, preferring to leave the range unoccupied, a buffer between them and their off-and-on enemy, the Catawbas. White settlers searching for new land usually bypassed these mountains, too, following the Catawba River or the Shenandoah Valley to gaps in the Blue Ridge that led farther west. Though a few homesites were established in these hills, and though all but the steepest slopes have been logged at least once, the South Mountains remained generally inaccessible and undeveloped until the 1930s, the domain of moonshiners, deer hunters, and trout fishermen.

The area began to change when the Civilian Conservation Corps established a camp in the South Mountains in 1933. Two hundred young men built roads into the region. They removed debris from the rivers and streambeds and constructed a fire tower. For the first time, the South Mountains were open to the public. But despite spectacular waterfalls, sparkling rivers and creeks, and some of the best views east of the Appalachians, the region continued to be ignored. It wasn't until 1974, when a state park was created, that the South Mountains got any attention at all. And though the area is only an hour's drive from Charlotte, North Carolina's largest metropolitan area, it's still not exactly crowded. In 1991, a year when Mount Mitchell State Park drew three hundred thousand tourists and the Smokies over eight million, the park at South Mountains had fewer than a hundred thousand visitors, many of them locals out for a Sunday-afternoon picnic or a short stroll. The result is a park that is as close to wilderness as any in the state system, a park for hikers and backpackers, for naturalists and seekers of solitude.

State Road 1904, the entrance road to South Mountains State Park, gives me the first clue to the nature of the park. It is a dusty, bumpy dirt track that, until improved in 1983, was suitable only for four-wheel-drive vehicles. It's better now, but it's still no interstate. The second clue comes in the parking lot, nearly empty on a sunshiny morning in late June. The final clue comes from Walter Gravely, the park's young, slim, down-home superintendent. Gravely loves this park and knows every inch of its 7,225 acres. He looks me over, glances at the walk I have planned, and immediately suggests a longer, more difficult route, one leg of which follows a "trail" from the top of High Shoals Falls to the bottom. Exactly why this "trail" is a clue to the wilderness character of the park will become clearer later, as will my reason for enclosing the word in quotation marks.

Diane, my wife, is with me today, and we begin on Head-quarters Trail, an old gravel logging road which crosses the park and parallels the clean, fast-flowing waters of Jacob's Fork. A tenth of a mile later, a sign points to a half-dozen log steps that lead to Chestnut Knob Trail. We take the stairs and begin to climb north out of the valley. Even though a heavy rain fell here last night, the trail is dry and soft and easy on the feet. It was built to last, too—or at least the stairs were. They were hand-cut from black-locust logs, a wood that mountaineers say outlasts stone.

The trail enters a second-growth forest of sizable tulip poplars, red maples, Fraser magnolias, and dogwoods. Pines begin to appear among the hardwoods. Towering white pines and substantial shortleaf pines grow along this trail, but as the path rises toward the ridge, three other species become more abundant: pitch pine (*Pinus rigida*), scrub pine (*Pinus virginiana*), and table mountain pine (*Pinus pungens*). These pines don't tower over anything; they are runts and are not thought to be good for much, the bastards at the pine-family reunion.

Pitch pine is the stunted, resiny tree of the New Jersey pine barrens. It rarely reaches fifty feet in height and is easily recognized by its stiff, dark needles. Its wood is coarse-grained, knotty, and hard to work, but the early colonists still found it useful. In 1709, John Lawson wrote that the wood of the pitch pine "(being replete with an abundance of *Bitumen*) is so durable that it seems to suffer no Decay, tho exposed to all Weathers, for many ages; and is used in several Domestick and Plantation Uses." One use was in the waterwheels of early America. The high resin content of the pitch pine makes it water repellent and rot resistant even under such wet conditions.

The scrub pine, with its irregular, drooping crown and dull green needles, appears to be even more useless to man than the pitch pine. Its wood warps easily and is suitable only for the roughest lumber or firewood or pulp. But in the Piedmont, where virtually every square foot of land has at one time or another been logged or farmed, the scrub pine is actually an important tree. This modest little evergreen is a great colonizer of old fields, readily germinating in the dry, eroded soils left behind by the plantation system of farming and the devastating logging practices once so prevalent in the South. As the years pass, the scrub pine is gradually succeeded by the more glamorous and economically important hardwoods, but without this pioneer, the process would take longer.

As the trail continues its climb up the south-facing slope toward the ridge line, the ground becomes rockier, and the chestnut oak, also known as mountain oak or rock oak, becomes more common. Ecologists know this forest of stubby pines and chestnut oaks as a xeric forest—the climax forest of the dry slopes and ridges of the Piedmont. It is supposed to be a common forest in the South, but this is the best example I've ever encountered, so we slow down to take it in better. Southern red oaks and a few hickories also grow here, as well as an occasional patch of mountain laurel and rhododendron. Wild irises and galax have sprouted beside the trail, but the most common trailside shrubs—and the real reason we slowed down—are the blueberries. Sunny patches of ground along the trail are carpeted with blueberry bushes, and since most of the berries are not quite ripe, it takes some hunting to find the few that are. But we manage to collect a handful, and they are sweet and delicious.

At the top of the ridge, Sawtooth Trail follows the ridge line to a spur trail that leads south to Chestnut Knob. The knob itself is a rocky outcrop almost bare of vegetation, with just a few stunted, beat-up-looking pines clinging to patches of soil here and there. It is a scene so reminiscent of the rocky promontories of the Monterey Peninsula in California that I half expect to see the Pacific Ocean crashing against the rocks. Instead, I look down on a lovely green valley and across it to a range of heavily forested hills. I examine one of the pines. Its needles are short and dark green, prickly to the touch. It is not, of course, a Monterey pine, but a pine of the rocky, wind-swept ridges of the East, an Appalachian exclusive—the table mountain pine.

André Michaux named the tree after Table Mountain in North Carolina, where he first saw them. The unassuming little pine didn't impress the great botanist; it had, he wrote, "no valuable properties to recommend it to notice in Europe." Perhaps so, but I love this defiant little tree that hangs on in places where even lichen has a hard time. I also like its nickname, the poverty pine. The origin of that name is obscure, but I'll bet it didn't come from a famous French botanist but rather from early settlers in these mountains, perhaps from a family trying to eke out a living on the steep slopes of some hardscrabble farm. A family whose companions were poverty and table mountain pines.

The next leg of the walk crosses the valley and climbs to a ridge on the other side. From there, the trail begins a steady descent to Shinny (pronounced Shiny, as in moonshine) Creek. Near the end of Possum Trail, a bridge leads across the creek. A few minutes later, we come to another crossing. No bridge spans this one, however, so we strip off our boots and wade. It's been a long, warm day, and the cold water rejuvenates our tired feet.

The forest near the creek is as different from the one along the ridge line as a tall, straight tulip poplar is from a gnarled and ancient table mountain pine. The difference, of course, is water. Down here, near the creek, there is plenty of it, so mountain laurel and rhododendron replace the blueberries we saw along the drier trail, and huge hemlocks and sweet gums stand in for the scrub pines and chestnut oaks.

From Shinny Creek, Cut-off Trail begins a steep climb to the top of High Shoals Falls. Tulip poplars and maples, ferns and trillium grow on this moist, north-facing slope. And though it's well past noon, the air is cooler than it was this morning on Chestnut Knob Trail.

At the top of the falls, someone has stacked a pile of lumber, so we find seats on the two-by-fours and watch broad, fast-flowing Jacob's Fork pour over a huge, smooth rock and vanish—literally vanish into the air. From up here, it's hard to tell if there really is a waterfall or whether the stream is just being sucked noisily into the vacuum of another dimension. I get as close to the edge as I can. The roar grows louder, but all I can see is a patch of white water in a small cascade just below the lip of the falls. Beyond that, there is nothing but emptiness.

We look for the trail that leads down the falls. One path peters out on a huge rock that an ant couldn't crawl down. A second one circles through the woods away from Jacob's Fork and winds up on an old logging road that leads farther away from the falls. By the time we get back to the upper falls, we've spent an hour looking for the missing trail. I decide to wade the river—which is thirty to forty feet wide and of undetermined depth—to search for a trail on the other side. Diane looks doubtful and decides to backtrack to an old road she noticed on the way up to the falls. I find a likely ford, drink the last of my water, and wearily take off my boots for the second time today. Then I think of the falls, just yards downstream, of the nothing-ness into which the river pours, of the lateness of the day, of the deserted woods around me. Elisha Mitchell's death at a water-fall near his eponymous mountain comes to mind, as well as the old saw about discretion and valor. I relace my boots and join Diane on Upper Falls Trail.

Less than half a mile later, we find an unsigned road that leads north, in the general direction of Shinny Creek. We walk down the gentle grade almost to the creek, to a sign that points back to the base of High Shoals Falls. I know exactly where I am: this is the trail I'd planned to take before Walter Gravely suggested a different route. I make a note to talk to Gravely when I get back.

This route to the lower falls parallels Jacob's Fork and leads upstream. Some teenagers who have been working on the trail point out a copperhead next to the path. It's a small snake, maybe two feet long. We would have walked right by it if the kids hadn't shown us where it was. The South Mountains are famous for their copperheads, and I'm happy to have a chance to see one. The kids, some of whom have been working in the creek and are barefoot, aren't so happy, and neither is Diane. They hustle on by and leave the snake to me. I squat down to get a better look. I see a big head, two unblinking eyes, and a body so well camouflaged that it seems to dissolve into the rocks on which it is coiled.

The copperhead (*Agkistrodon contortrix*) is a member of the pit viper family, made up of over two hundred species of snakes that are distributed throughout the world. The family name comes from the small, heat-sensing pits located between the eyes and nostrils. The pits aid the snakes in detecting warm-blooded prey, but the one I'm watching needs no such help; it's staring directly at me.

Copperheads are gray, heavy-bodied snakes with brown hour-glass markings and triangular heads that are larger than their necks. They are found throughout the East from Massachusetts to Florida, and they are very common in North Carolina. They are also responsible for most of the poisonous snakebites report-

ed in the state. For that reason, copperheads get a bad rap. People deliberately run over them with their cars and chop them to pieces with garden hoes. But they are not aggressive snakes and will strike only when touched—and sometimes not even then. Most bites occur when someone accidentally steps on one. And though such bites are serious and require prompt medical attention, they are rarely, if ever, fatal.

I break off the staring contest with the copperhead and rejoin Diane in the climb to the falls. This part of the trail is within spitting distance of the river. Water rushes over and around Volkswagen-sized boulders; the path becomes rocky and rough, and the rumble of the falls grows louder.

At the bottom of High Shoals Falls, an observation platform

looks out over a ravine which Jacob's Fork has carved out of rock and soil. A spectacular torrent of water, an elongated cylinder of pure silver, drops eighty feet into a churning pool. The drop is nearly vertical, which explains why the falls are invisible from the top. Rainbows form and disappear in the mist. The air is cool. I am enchanted with the falls, but before leaving, I study the rock face of the cliff over which it pours. If there is a trail down from the top of the falls, I can't see it. A mountain goat would have trouble with those eighty feet. I write another note. "See Gravely about path down falls," it says.

We walk back down to Shinny Creek and finish the last half-mile to the parking lot in a fog of exhaustion. After drinking a quart of water from a cooler in the car, I stagger over to the office. A man in a spiffy park uniform is standing outside.

"Gravely around?" I ask.

"No," the man replies, "he's gone for the day."

I haul out the map on which Gravely traced his suggested route. "See this? Gravely penciled in this route. It was a great walk until we got to the top of the falls, but where is the path down? We couldn't find anything resembling a trail."

"There isn't one," he says.

"No trail?"

"No. We have miles of easy, well-marked trails here, but there's still some rough country left, too. Gravely wouldn't have told you about the shortcut down the falls if he didn't think you were experienced enough for a scramble. What happened?"

I hesitate. "Ah, nothing much," I say finally. "Just wasted some time trying to find a way down."

"That's the way it is with South Mountains," he says. "When

you go into a wilderness, even a small wilderness like this one, life *should* get a little unpredictable."

It's been a warm day, but a faint chill in the air announces that sundown is near. My sweat-soaked shirt feels cool against my skin. I sit down on the porch steps and enjoy the pleasant tiredness that follows a good, long walk. "Right," I say. "I wouldn't want it any other way."

Before You Go

For More Information
South Mountains State Park
Route 1, Box 206-C
Connelly Springs, N.C. 28612
(704) 433-4772

Accommodations
Burke County Chamber of Commerce
110 East Meeting Street
Morganton, N.C. 28655
(704) 437-3021

Campgrounds
Eleven family campsites with picnic tables and fire circles are located 0.5 mile east of the park office just off State Road 1904, the entrance road to South Mountains State Park. The park also has four primitive campgrounds for backpackers, with a total of fourteen campsites. All four campgrounds are situated in mountain meadows and are stocked with an abundance of split firewood.

Maps
In a more perfect world, the free park map is all you would need for this walk, but vandals removed some of the park's trail signs sometime

before I took this walk, so you might want to take along a compass for backup.

Additional Reading

"An Appalachian Original" by Charles E. Williams, *American Forests* 98, July-August 1992, 24–26.

Common Forest Trees of North Carolina, 15th ed., originally prepared by J. S. Holmes, North Carolina Department of Natural Resources, Division of Forest Products, Raleigh, 1983.

The Geology of the Carolinas edited by J. Wright Horton, Jr., and Victor A. Zullo, University of Tennessee Press, Knoxville, 1991.

A Natural History of Trees of Eastern and Central North America by Donald Culross Peattie, Houghton Mifflin Company, Boston, 1948.

A New Voyage to Carolina by John Lawson, edited with an introduction and notes by Hugh Talmage Lefler, University of North Carolina Press, Chapel Hill, 1967.

"The Quiet Majesty of South Mountains" by Kay Scott, *Wildlife in North Carolina* 53, August 1989, 24–27.

A Sierra Club Naturalist's Guide to the Piedmont by Michael A. Godfrey, Sierra Club Books, San Francisco, 1980.

Snakes of Eastern North America by Carl H. Ernst and Roger W. Barbour, George Mason University Press, Fairfax, Va., 1989.

Length: 7.3 miles

**Degree
of Difficulty: Moderate**

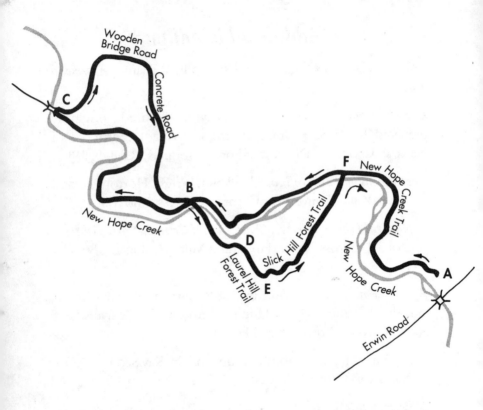

New Hope Creek Trail

A. New Hope Creek Trail begins here.
B. First bridge across New Hope Creek
C. Second bridge across New Hope Creek
D. Intersection of New Hope Creek Trail
    and Laurel Hill Forest Trail
E. Intersection of Laurel Hill Forest Trail
    and Slick Hill Forest Trail
F. Intersection of Slick Hill Forest Trail
    and New Hope Creek Trail

Route and Distances

A. to C.	New Hope Creek Trail	3.3 mi.
C. to B.	Wooden Bridge Road	
	and Concrete Road	1.5 mi.
B. to D.	New Hope Creek Trail	0.3 mi.
D. to E.	Laurel Hill Forest Trail	0.4 mi.
E. to F.	Slick Hill Forest Trail	0.7 mi.
F. to A.	New Hope Creek Trail	1.1 mi.

TOTAL 7.3 mi.

A Mostly Managed Forest

New Hope Creek Trail
Duke Forest

Erwin Road runs between Chapel Hill and Durham. It crosses New Hope Creek about midway between the two towns. A gated entrance to Duke Forest lies a few feet north of the creek. From the trailhead, follow New Hope Creek Trail 3.3 miles to the second bridge. The trail vanishes in spots, and although you can pick your way through on either side of the creek, the north side is generally easier. From the second bridge, proceed north on Wooden Bridge Road, then south on Concrete Road. Cross New Hope Creek at Concrete Road Bridge and pick up the trail that runs along the south side of the creek. Follow it to Laurel Hill Forest Trail. Stay on Laurel Hill until you reach Slick Hill Trail. Follow Slick Hill Trail back to New Hope Creek Trail. From the trail junction, it is a little over 1 mile back to the trailhead.

*D*uke University owns the 7,700-acre Duke Forest. The university's students and faculty conduct forestry research projects there, and they ask recreational users to take special precautions (see the "Before You Go" section). But the restrictions are minor, and the

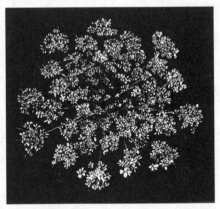

forest's thirty-five miles of gravel roads and trails make it an ideal place for walkers and naturalists to explore the Piedmont.

The forest is split into six divisions. I chose a walk in the Korstian Division because almost half the trail is along New Hope Creek. This route gives the walker over three miles of dense, unmanaged alluvial forest to scramble through and contrast with the return route, which is primarily on roads through farmland that was once scarred by abuse. This is land that is healing itself, reverting to forest, in some sections by natural seeding, in others with the help of the employees and students of Duke's School of the Environment (formerly called the School of Forestry).

I take this walk one morning in September when a dry spell has reduced New Hope Creek to a trickle. As soon as the road noise is behind me, I hear the first *thwap*! It is a sound that will follow me along the entire creek, the first shot in the Great Hickory Nut Bombardment. Although I don't see one of the bombardiers for another half-mile, I know who's responsible: *Sciurus carolinensis*, the terror of the backyard bird feeder, known to most of us as the eastern gray squirrel.

When Europeans first settled this area in the mid-eighteenth century, gray squirrels were so common and so destructive to crops that some townships paid a bounty for their hides. But as the forests disappeared, so did the squirrels, and by 1900 they were so scarce their survival was in doubt.

Biologists attribute their abundance today to forest-management practices that have encouraged the spread of hardwood forests—the climax forest of the Piedmont. Gray squirrels prefer mature stands of beech, oak, and hickory. They nest in cavities in these trees or build large nests of twigs and leaves in their branches. They shun pines and rarely nest in them. And since pines are usually the first trees to recolonize cleared land, few squirrels are found in the early stages of successional forests. But the land along New Hope Creek is too steep and too rocky to farm, and it is lined today—as it has been for centuries—with mature sycamores and beeches, oaks and hickories. *Thwap!*

Much of this trail is within a few feet of New Hope Creek. Black-eyed Susans brighten the streamside, and frogs sun themselves on the banks. They announce my coming with a loud *ribbit*, followed by a pause and an emphatic splash. Turtles slide quietly into the clear, nearly still water.

In addition to the acorns and hickory nuts scattered near the trail, I find an occasional black walnut. Duke Forest, it turns out, is home to the largest recorded black walnut tree still standing in North Carolina. Black walnuts—once common in the bottomland forests of the Piedmont—are hard to come by these days. A single large tree can be worth over twenty thousand dollars to its lucky owner. The wood is cut into wafer-thin slices to veneer furniture, or it is chopped into solid chunks for machining into stocks for fine rifles and shotguns.

Early settlers weren't as persnickety in their use of the wood. They used black walnut for everything from railroad ties to cradles. It also made the finest cabinet wood of any North American tree, and millions of board feet were exported to England to be used in furniture. Because of its great value, the black walnut was nearly expunged from American forests. And since it takes a forest-grown tree a hundred years or more to reach maturity, it'll be awhile—even in protected areas like this—before the towering black walnuts of yesteryear will be seen in anything like their previous numbers.

Since the rough black shells that guard the walnuts' delicious meat have the approximate hardness of diamond, I was surprised to learn that squirrels *love* to eat them. I've tried to crack the shells with everything from a sledgehammer to a bench vise, and to think that a half-pound rodent can chisel them apart with ease is astonishing. Of course, squirrels have always amazed me. Irritated me, too, on occasion. Many times, I've seen one walk coolly down a pine tree, cartwheel ten feet through the air, land on a smooth metal baffle, slide slowly down it until its feet reach the top of my squirrel-proof bird feeder, devour a ton or two of pricey sunflower seed, then go back the way it came, all the while ignoring my screams of outrage. *Thwap!*

In places along this creek, rocky bluffs rise fifty to seventy-five feet above the water and squeeze the stream into narrow gorges. The water moves more swiftly there, and the trail detours up and around the headlands. The farther upstream I go, the less defined the detours become. After passing Concrete Road Bridge, I find myself bushwhacking around some of the bluffs, in one spot pulling myself up a steep hill by grabbing rhododendron bushes that lie thickly on the slope. Several times I cross the creek, from the north side to the south side and back again, to find the easiest route. Huge boulders choke the streambed and dead trees lie across it, making the crossings easy at low water. Gnawed tree stumps indicate that beavers are plentiful, but there are no dams.

Later, I stop by Duke's School of the Environment to see Judson Edeburn, who manages the forest for the university, to find out why. "Don't be fooled," he warns. "New Hope Creek can flood suddenly after a thunderstorm or heavy rains. I've seen the bridges under water many times. No beaver dam in the world could hold that creek during high water." Nor would my crisscrossing technique work. If you walk this trail during high water, I suggest staying on the north side of the creek. On the whole, it's the easier trail.

And by the time I reach Wooden Bridge Road, I'm ready for an easier trail. I've beaten my way through enough Piedmont alluvial forest for one day. I clamber up to the roadway and head north on a pleasant, well-graded dirt road. The change is remarkable and refreshing, the scenery ever-varying. This road runs through the working part of Duke Forest, its reason for being.

The university began acquiring the land for Duke Forest in the mid-1920s to buffer its new main campus from the outside world. By 1931, it had purchased nearly five thousand acres, most of it abandoned farmland. The school asked Dr. Clarence F. Korstian, a well-known silviculturist who later became the first dean of Duke's School of Forestry, to manage it. He agreed and decided to run the forest as a business where "students and forest-land owners can see the actual results of investigations and forestry practice."

The raw material he had to work with didn't amount to much. Much of the land was "farmed-out," a condition Korstian described in the June 1935 issue of the *Duke University Forestry Bulletin*:

> *Under the plantation system of southern agriculture, each estate was essentially a self-sustaining economic unit. . . . Under this system, which involved clearing large areas of forest land and placing it under cultivation, little attention was given to the maintenance of soil fertility. Land was plentiful, labor was cheap, and when the top soil of a field had been washed from the slopes or when the land no longer produced a satisfactory agricultural crop, it was "turned out" and allowed to revert to forest, and new*

fertile land was cleared and put under cultivation. Many stands of second-growth timber 10 to 70 years old occur in the Duke Forest on land which was at one time under cultivation, as shown by the old corn or cotton rows which are still discernible.

As I walk the roads and fire trails of the forest, a sense of well-being emanates from the land. Its contours are rounded, gentle, and healthy. It seems to be saying that this is what will happen if you treat me properly, with respect. Not that Duke Forest is a wilderness—this land is being farmed, and its product is trees. But it's being farmed carefully and intelligently, and the land is responding well. In his essay "The Making of a Marginal Farm," Wendell Berry described reclaiming worn-out land for his farm in Kentucky. How, year by year, the land became healthier, more productive. This is the sort of farm Korstian and his successors have created. And a walk through it is a pleasure to be remembered.

The last leg of the walk takes me back to New Hope Creek. The sun is out, and puff balls of mud rise slowly in the sluggishly moving water as small creatures, hearing me coming, bury themselves in the bottom of the stream. Light-footed water bugs dimple the surface of stagnant pools. There are deer, wild turkey, and foxes in this forest, but all I seem to bump into are squirrels. *Thwap! Thwap!* Two neatly separated quarters of a hickory nut's green outer husk fall at my feet.

Squirrels are particularly busy in September, when they begin laying in nuts for the cold months ahead. Sometimes, they drop the whole fruit from a hickory tree and follow it to the ground, where they husk it and bury the hard-shelled nut; other times, they husk the fruit in the tree and scamper to the ground with full cheek pouches to cache the nuts. This behavior enables the squirrels to survive the Piedmont winters; it also plays an important role in the spread of hardwood forests.

The seeds of most trees are light enough that wind and birds can carry them to new areas to propagate the species. But nuts and acorns are too heavy, and naturalists believe that squirrels perform this function for nut-bearing species. Although they are remarkably good at finding their buried nuts, even gray squirrels forget occasionally. And since the depth they choose to cache their winter supplies is the optimum depth for germination, a single amnesic *Sciurus* can become the Johnny Appleseed of oaks and walnuts and hickories.

Near the end of the trail, just before you reach the road, there is a partial dam across the creek, a five-foot-high rock wall that starts on the south bank and extends three-quarters of the way to the north bank. It's hard to see it when you're walking upstream, but it's almost impossible to miss it on your return. The structure was built to create a millrace—the strong current needed to turn the waterwheel of a gristmill. Time has erased any trace of the mill that must have once stood here, but the dam—like the old furrows that can still be seen in the loblolly-pine tracts set out by Dr. Korstian—still exists. Duke Forest, like all land, is a palimpsest with the scrawl of ancient hands still partially visible. The trick is to remember that we are writing today on the same parchment and that what we write will be with the land for a long time.

Before You Go

For More Information

Duke Forest
School of the Environment
Duke University
Durham, N.C. 27706
(919) 684-2421

Accommodations

Durham Visitors Center
P.O. Box 3536
Durham, N.C. 27702
(800) 448-8604

Campgrounds

There are no campsites in Duke Forest. The nearest public campsites are at Eno River State Park.

Maps

Maps of Duke Forest are available from the School of the Environment for a small fee. New Hope Creek Trail is not on the map, nor is it maintained. But it does exist, and it's easy to follow—at least in most places. The roads and foot trails in the rest of the forest are well marked and well maintained, but a map will help you navigate them.

Special Precautions

Although it is almost impossible to get lost on New Hope Creek Trail, it is a little rough, and I would not recommend it for children.

Because the forest is used for research projects, the School of the Environment asks recreational users to follow ten simple rules listed in its brochure "Duke Forest." The rules are sensible and similar to England's "Country Code." Two particularly important ones forbid access to the forest after sundown and prohibit cutting, picking, or damaging the vegetation in any way.

Points of Interest _____

Many other walks are possible in Duke Forest; this is one of the more challenging. If you're looking for a Sunday-afternoon stroll, you can easily find one if you have a map.

Additional Reading

"The Duke Forest: A Demonstration and Research Laboratory" by Clarence F. Korstian, *Duke University Forestry Bulletin* 1, June 1935, 9.

Mammals of the Carolinas, Virginia, and Maryland by William David Webster, James F. Parnell, and Walter C. Biggs, Jr., University of North Carolina Press, Chapel Hill, 1985.

A Natural History of Trees of Eastern and Central North America by Donald Culross Peattie, Houghton Mifflin Company, Boston, 1948.

A Sierra Club Naturalist's Guide to the Piedmont by Michael A. Godfrey, Sierra Club Books, San Francisco, 1980.

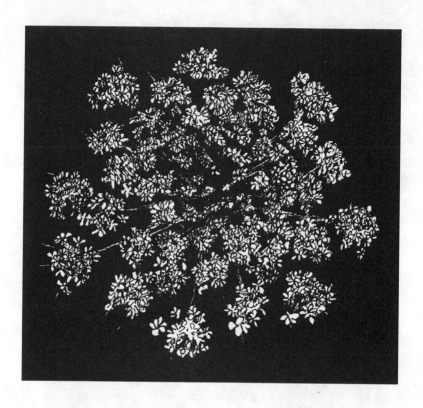

Pettigrew State Park

THE COASTAL PLAIN

*There are great flocks of these
[wild turkeys] in* Carolina. *I
have seen about five hundred in
a Flock; some of them are very
large. I never weigh'd any
myself, but have been inform'd
of one that weigh'd near sixty
Pound Weight. I have seen half
a Turkey feed eight hungry
Men two Meals.*

John Lawson, 1709

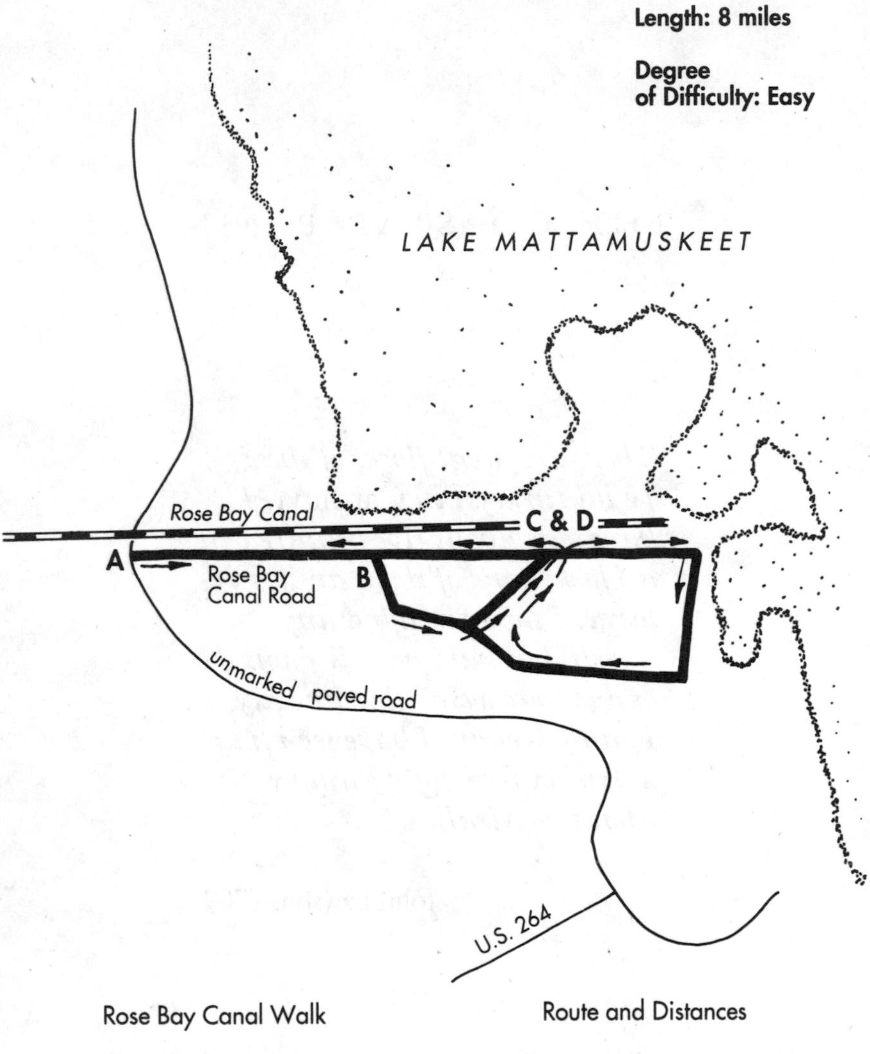

Length: 8 miles

Degree
of Difficulty: Easy

LAKE MATTAMUSKEET

Rose Bay Canal

C & D

A

Rose Bay
Canal Road

B

unmarked paved road

U.S. 264

Rose Bay Canal Walk

A.   Trailhead
B.   Intersection with road around
       first impoundment
C., D. Road around second
       impoundment begins and
       ends here.

Route and Distances

A. to B.	Rose Bay Canal Dike	0.6 mi.
B. to C.	Walk around first impoundment	1.8 mi.
C. to D.	Circle second impoundment	3.2 mi.
D. to A.	Return to trailhead	2.4 mi.

TOTAL 8.0 mi.

The Tundra Swan Walk

Rose Bay Canal
Mattamuskeet National Wildlife Refuge

Mattamuskeet National Wildlife Refuge is located north of Swan Quarter in Hyde County. An unnamed, unnumbered road splits off from U.S. 264 and circles the lake. Rose Bay Canal is at the road's westernmost point. There's a gate into the refuge, along with parking for two or three cars. From the gate, walk east on the Jeep road that parallels Rose Bay Canal. Proceed counterclockwise around the first impoundment and continue east on Rose Bay Canal Road until it ends at the lake. Walk clockwise on the road around the second impoundment, then return west along Rose Bay Canal Road to the trailhead.

A great peat fire hollowed out a basin in the earth which later filled with rainwater, creating the lake now called Mattamuskeet. Or so one theory goes. Another proclaims that the lake is the largest of the Carolina bays, those shallow depressions that mar the sandy flatness of the southern Atlantic coastal plain like pockmarks on an adolescent's cheek. Some scientists believe the bays were formed by a long-ago meteorite shower. Others think they were shaped during the last Ice Age by the action of strong, unidirectional winds on the shallow ponds of the region. But however obscure its origin, North Carolina's largest natural lake is an important landmark. And one with a clear natu-

ral function: it's the winter home of 150,000 migratory water-fowl.

If you drive eastward toward the lake, you'll notice the fields getting larger, the towns getting smaller. This is agribusiness country, dominated by huge farms, and in winter most of them are gray and bare, stark shadows of summer's ripeness. But a few have been planted with winter wheat, and as you near the lake, you will start to see white specks in those improbable emerald-green fields. The specks are tundra swans, large, all-white birds that winter in this area.

Aside from the occasional green field and the bleak browns of winter stubble, another color will gradually impose itself on you. The closer you get to the lake, the more obvious it becomes. The color is black, and it comes from the soil, soil so rich that it begs for cultivation. Seeing forty thousand acres of that soil covered by a skim of water has irritated farmers since the nineteenth century. And their attempts to drain it to get at the lake's fertile bottom have made up most of Mattamuskeet's written history.

The idea of draining the lake has been around since the early 1800s, but it wasn't until 1909, when the North Carolina Board of Education sold 48,830 acres to the Southern Land Reclamation Company, that work actually got started. The price was two dollars an acre, and the property included Lake Mattamuskeet. The farmers had been right about the soil; a survey by the Department of Agriculture stated that the lake bottom would be as productive as any land in the state and would require no fertilizer for the first several years of cultivation.

Bids were let for a pumping station, and a building with a

125-foot-tall smokestack was constructed. The cost was thirty thousand dollars. The old power plant is still standing and in remarkably good condition. You can see it near the headquarters of the refuge. It's easy to find; just look for the smokestack.

The big money, however, went for dredging drainage canals and for eight centrifugal pumps and the four 850-horsepower steam engines that drove them. It was a big, complex project. Inevitably, there were delays, and the pumps didn't begin pumping until 1916. By then, the Southern Land Reclamation Company had changed its name to New Holland Farms, in honor of a similar drainage project carried out in the Netherlands. The name change didn't help; although the company succeeded in draining the lake, the seven-year undertaking mortally wounded its finances, and in 1918 it sold the lake bed to the North Carolina Farms Company.

The new company managed to farm only a thousand acres before 1923, when it went into receivership. But it was the Roaring Twenties, times were good, so optimism prevailed. Yet a third company—the New Holland Corporation—was formed to try again.

By the time the pumps were restored in 1926, rainwater had refilled the lake, but it took only a few months to empty it again. A prison camp was built nearby to supply cheap labor, and serious farming finally got under way. In 1928, a heavy thunderstorm ruined 1,500 acres of wheat. In 1929, the project manager went home to Massachusetts for Christmas and never returned. Even so, by 1932, 12,000 acres were in production. But the country was in the grip of the Depression by then, and the company was losing money on every acre. That year, the farmers gave up for good, and the huge pumps went silent for the last time.

Two years later, the New Holland Corporation sold 49,925 acres of land and lake to the United States government. The property was designated a national wildlife refuge. The pumps were sold for scrap, and the pump house was converted into a lodge for hunters, which continued to operate until 1974.

The New Holland Corporation died quickly; it left its final crop standing in the lake bed, which refilled quickly. The corporation also left eighty-three miles of canals, most of which still exist. And the dikes built to create those canals make fine, flat trails which today's walker can use to explore the margins of the lake.

The walk I prefer starts at the Rose Bay Canal gate at the western end of the lake. The trail is a narrow, limited-access dirt road the refuge staff uses to check water levels and waterfowl populations. It parallels the canal and circles two large impoundments which the refuge built in the mid-1960s to enhance the habitat for wintering waterfowl. The trail also passes the northern edge of the 153-acre Salyer's Ridge Natural Area—a grove of mature loblolly pines so thick that its canopy shuts out most of the light, keeping out understory and leaving the forest floor mulched with a soft bed of pine straw that a professional landscaper would envy.

Winter—December, January, and early February are best—is the time to take this walk, because that's when waterfowl populations are at their peak. In summer, you will see fewer birds—and a lot of mosquitoes the size of birds.

I've walked these dikes several times, but the walk I remember best was one raw, overcast morning in February. As I headed east along the dike, the noise grew, a cacophony of *hoos* and *hoots* and *gabbles*. Back in the early sixties when a hundred thousand Canada geese wintered at Mattamuskeet, one writer reported that you could hear them twenty miles from the lake. These days, most of the geese don't make it this far south. As more food became available—waste corn, primarily—they began short-stopping, wintering on the Delmarva Peninsula and at points north. So it's quieter now, but not much.

The first impoundment is a mile from the gate. On that morning, it was packed with tundra swans, graceful, long-necked birds with wingspreads of six or seven feet. My presence alarmed the flock closest to me, and the birds flapped heavily into the air, forming a silvery, scraggly V. The sounds coming from the lake became louder and higher pitched as the remaining swans expressed their resentment at being disturbed. I sank to the ground and didn't move. After a while, the swans settled down again, and I eased my binoculars out of my knapsack to watch them.

The tundra swan (*Olor columbianus*), the common swan of North America, was known as the whistling swan until its name was changed by the American Ornithologists' Union a few years ago. The new adjective fits better, because the tundra is where these birds spend much of their time. They nest from the Seward Peninsula in Alaska north to the Arctic Slope and east to northern Canada. About half of them make it to the Atlantic flyway, while the others winter in the West, opting for the easier commute down to San Francisco Bay and California's Central Valley.

To reach Mattamuskeet, these swans have put in some long hours at high altitudes. Pilots have reported seeing them a mile up. On their trip south, they fly night and day with few rest

stops. And by the time they settle in for the winter, they're hungry.

For thousands of years, the swans and geese of North America fed exclusively on aquatic vegetation—on widgeon grass and wild celery and sago pondweed. Then, sometime in the last one hundred years, some goose Einstein figured out that corn and soybeans and winter wheat were easier pickings. Swans, apparently slower on the uptake, didn't pick up on this until about 1970. Since then, they've also become confirmed field feeders, flying out at dawn to glean waste corn and soybeans and gray winter wheat from nearby farms.

Some traditionalists remain, however, and I watched them going about their ancient business on the impoundment. They were using their long necks to browse the bottom, keeping their heads underwater for prolonged periods. From a distance, the feeding swans appeared inert, more like headless rafts of white feathers than birds. Then a head would pop up, and—like the ugly duckling—a graceless blob would be transformed into a majestic swan.

More than 45,000 tundra swans wintered at Mattamuskeet during the 1990–91 season, but swans are only the spectacular tip of the lake's wildlife. A hundred thousand ducks also dropped in: pintails and mallards, canvasbacks and widgeons, ruddy ducks, mergansers, scaup, and more. Over twenty species of ducks have been spotted on the lake, not to mention the cormorants and loons that also winter there.

As I continued around the impoundment, several flocks of ducks flushed from the water and the woods. Then four white-tailed deer raised their flags and made a mad dash across the shallow water, moving so fast that they left a white wake trailing behind them. Their noisy exit caused the entire impoundment to erupt; ducks and geese and swans labored into the air, their feathers flashing dully in the weak sun as they gained altitude and flew off with steady, measured wingbeats.

I followed the path around the impoundment until it rejoined Rose Bay Canal. On the road that parallels the canal, I headed east toward the second, larger impoundment. At its southeastern tip—on the part of the walk farthest from the entrance gate—while three coot fluttered halfheartedly down a canal pretending to run from me, I glimpsed a black form on the bank and heard its heavy splash. Seconds later, a head popped up. An otter peered curiously at me for a moment, then vanished silently.

Later, halfway around the impoundment, six red-tailed hawks spiraled lazily over a dozen egrets that were fishing the flats in front of me. On that same walk, I saw a pointy-winged hawk with a narrow tail that I think was a peregrine falcon; an osprey on its nest; and a great blue heron stalking fish in a canal. I saw wood ducks floating like brightly painted decoys in the shallow water and green-winged teal overhead. Near the road, an overweight Canada goose waddled through a field of millet. And I saw only a fraction of what Mattamuskeet offers.

After finishing the walk, I stopped by to see Kelly Davis, the wildlife biologist for the refuge. She's pretty and blond, and in her eleven years there, she has seen all of the lake and most of its inhabitants: black bear and bobcats; ten species of turtles and more of snakes; anhingas and snow geese; bald eagles; and, once, a golden eagle.

Hyde County has no incorporated cities or towns and a population of 5,411. It has its own rough beauty, but urban it isn't. Davis is from Ohio, and I wondered how she felt about living in this watery, sparsely populated land of small towns and big farms. When I asked her how much longer she wanted to stay at Mattamuskeet, she looked at me curiously, wondering what prompted the question. Then she thought for a moment. "Forever," she said finally. "I'd like to stay here forever."

Before You Go

For More Information _____
Mattamuskeet National Wildlife Refuge
Route 1, Box N-2
Swan Quarter, N.C. 27885
(919) 926-4021

Accommodations _____
Greater Hyde County Chamber of Commerce
Engelhard, N.C. 27824

Campgrounds

Camping is not permitted in the refuge. The nearest public campgrounds are at Pettigrew State Park and Goose Creek State Park.

Maps

The map in the refuge's free brochure is all you'll need for this walk.

Special Precautions

The refuge sets aside a few days each winter for waterfowl hunting; those are good days to avoid.

Points of Interest _____

The 16,411-acre Swanquarter National Wildlife Refuge is just off U.S. 264, southwest of Mattamuskeet. This refuge is on Pamlico Sound and is the winter home of large numbers of diving ducks. Most of it is accessible only by boat, but an 1,100-foot pier offers land-bound visitors a peek at this impressive refuge.

Additional Reading

Ducks, Geese and Swans of North America by Frank C. Bellrose, Stackpole Books, Harrisburg, Pa., 1976.

"An Overview of the History of Mattamuskeet Drainage District and the Efforts by Private Corporations to Reclaim the Lands Under the Waters of Lake Mattamuskeet for Productive Agricultural Purposes" by Lewis C. Forrest, in *Lake Mattamuskeet Lodge: Recommendations for Adaptive Reuse*, East Carolina University Regional Development Institute, Greenville, N.C., 1988

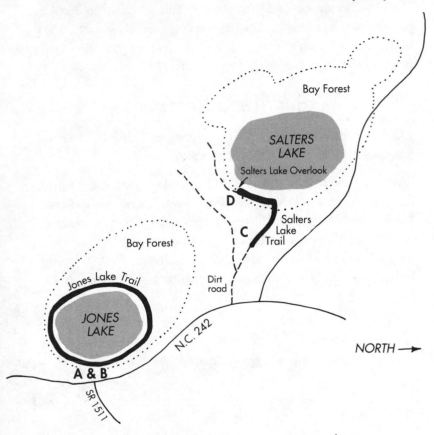

**Length: 4 miles
(total for both trails)**

**Degree
of Difficulty: Easy**

Bay Forest

*SALTERS
LAKE*

Salters Lake Overlook

D

C

Salters
Lake
Trail

Bay Forest

Jones Lake *Trail*

*JONES
LAKE*

Dirt
road

N.C. 242

NORTH →

A & B

SR 1511

Jones Lake and Salters Lake Trails

A., B.   Loop around Jones Lake
         begins and ends here.
C.   Walk to Salters Lake begins here.
D.   Salters Lake overlook

Route and Distances

A. to B.	Jones Lake Loop	2.8 mi.
C. to D.	Trail to Salters Lake overlook	0.6 mi.
D. to C.	Return	0.6 mi.
	TOTAL	4.0 mi.

Carolina Bays

Jones Lake–Salters Lake Trails
Jones Lake State Park

This walk has two legs—a loop trail around Jones Lake and a walk to Salters Lake. Jones Lake State Park is located 4 miles north of Elizabethtown on N.C. 242. Jones Lake Nature Trail begins at the northern corner of the park's picnic area. After 0.5 mile, the nature trail joins the loop trail that circles the lake, passing through a dense bay forest interspersed with cypress and juniper and longleaf pine. Salters Lake Trail starts in Bladen Lakes State Forest, a 2-mile drive from Jones Lake. To reach the unnamed road into Salters Lake, you must leave Jones Lake State Park and head north on N.C. 242. Turn left onto the first dirt road, located about 1 mile from the park. The first right, which is less than 0.5 mile from the dirt road, leads to Salters Lake. The walk begins on a white-sand road at a sign that reads "Closed to Vehicles." After 0.25 mile, the road reenters Jones Lake State Park and bears left through a pine savanna to Salters Lake. Return by the same route.

*O*ver half a million shallow depressions known as Carolina bays pit the otherwise smooth surface of the southern Atlantic coastal plain. These geological anomalies range in size from mere dimples to thousands of acres, and though scientists have investigated their every aspect, the story of the bays remains incomplete, awaiting a final chapter. This walk offers the hiker a chance to study these enigmatic bays and enjoy the unique ecosystem associated with them.

Although the bays are scattered from Maryland to Florida, they are called Carolina bays because their concentration is highest in North and South Carolina. All of the bays were once lakes, but vegetation has filled in most of them, leaving nearly impassable peat bogs. But a few relict bay lakes still exist, and they are nowhere more clustered and more accessible than in Bladen County, North Carolina. And since Jones Lake State Park is in the dead center of that county, there is no better place to begin to explore the bays and their geology than along the shores of the two Carolina bay lakes that lie within the park's boundaries.

I begin the three-mile loop around Jones Lake on a sunshiny morning in early spring. From the brightness of the park's grassy, open picnic area, I plunge into a dense, shadowy forest. The trail is black and wet, and the air has the slightly sweet smell of rotting vegetation. The sudden transition from civilization to forest is like stepping out of one of Seurat's parks into one of Rousseau's jungles.

But this is no jungle, this is a temperate-zone bay forest, one of the more unusual ecosystems in the South. Carolina bays, it turns out, are named not for their oval depressions but for the forests that occupy those depressions—forests filled with, among other things, bay trees. There are the aromatic red bays and bayberries. There are sweet bays, bull bays, and loblolly bays. Mixed in with the bays is a nearly impenetrable confusion of vines and fetterbush, swamp maples and red cedars. And above this Darwinian tangle of competing shrubs, bushes, and low-lying trees loom the cypresses, the longleaf pines, and the majestic Atlantic white cedars.

White cedar (*Chamaecyparis thyoides*) is better known in North Carolina as juniper. And though the eponymous bay trees interest me, it is the towering junipers, with their stringy spirals of red bark, that intrigue me the most. So when I find one just a few yards up the trail, I stop and stare upward, trying to pick out the blue-green canopy that I know must be there, somewhere above the bays.

Juniper forests once covered the peaty wetlands of the eastern United States from Maine to northern Florida, but the tree is much less common these days. In fact, the Nature Conservancy classifies white-cedar forests as a "globally endangered" habitat. The algorithm governing the trees' precipitous decline was the usual one: the more valuable a wild species is to man, the quicker it gets used up. And the juniper was a very valuable tree to the white settlers of North America.

Juniper wood splits easily and is very light; at twenty pounds per cubic foot, it has a density about half that of loblolly pine. And like most trees that grow in swamps, its wood is durable and resistant to rot. This combination of qualities made juniper important to the early colonists. They used its pleasantly scented wood for staves in their water barrels; they used it to build log cabins, they used it to plank boats, and most of all, they used this easy-to-split wood to shingle their houses. The demand was so great that as early as 1750, juniper was already considered scarce.

Of course, it wasn't scarce at all; only the easily accessible trees had been cut. The huge juniper forests of the Great Dismal Swamp and other peaty, hard-to-get-at wetlands—like the Carolina bays—lasted until the mid-nineteenth century, when the advent of steam dredges allowed lumbermen to drain those large, forbidding swamps and run railroads into them to haul out the logs. Today, Atlantic white cedars occupy less than 5 percent of their former acreage, and stands of mature trees are rarer than a spotted owl at a loggers' convention.

Beyond the juniper, a short trail leads to Jones Lake. Its white-sand bottom is clearly visible beneath the peat-stained, tea-brown water. A red cedar leans over the lake, searching for sunlight.

A little farther down the main trail, a wooden footbridge spans a narrow creek. In what appears to be a reversal of gravity, the waters of the stream are not flowing into the lake but out of it. I drop a stick into the water and watch it bob downstream and vanish in the forest. Jones Lake, it seems, is a lake on a hill, a pocosin in the making.

Pocosin is a common word in the books and pamphlets that describe the natural areas of eastern North Carolina. Most of them simply say that it is Indian for "swamp on a hill." The word probably comes from the Algonquian *pakwesen*, meaning "shallow place" or "place where there is a shallow." In any case, pocosins are densely vegetated, boglike wetlands, and Carolina bays are a specialized form of pocosin that have sand rims raised above the general level of the land around them. So the Indian definition of "swamp on a hill" fits the bays well. The overflow from heavy rains or a breach in the sand rim around a bay lake can account for a stream that flows in the wrong direction.

The vegetation along the shore of Jones Lake is almost identical to the flora found in Carolina bays without lakes in them. The reason is the soil. The boggy black dirt of the trail I am walking is compacted peat—the same material that fills most Carolina bays.

When vegetable matter—leaves, twigs, branches, and so forth—falls into stagnant water, it decomposes incompletely because of a lack of oxygen. With time and pressure, this half-rotted organic muck becomes peat. Although scientists are still arguing about what created the Carolina bays, they generally agree that the bays started life as impermeable depressions that filled with water. Over the centuries, as the forests surrounding them shed organic debris into the water, the lakes slowly filled in. Although some bays are only partially filled with peat—two-thirds of this bay, for example, is peat-filled, with Jones Lake occupying the remaining third—the process continues, and the result is an ever-diminishing lake surrounded by an ever-expanding circle of peat. Thus, as with all of the bay lakes, Jones Lake's fate is sealed: unless interfered with by man, its shoreline will continue to advance until the tightening noose of peat eventually chokes the lake out of existence.

Beyond the bridge and the wrong-way stream, the trail narrows and becomes rougher, a snarl of cypress knees and roots. I duck under large vines and catbriers that dangle over the trail. I hear the cries of ducks and the songs of birds I can't identify.

About halfway around the lake, the forest recedes, and the trail passes through a thorny jungle of waist-high brush. For the first time since I entered the bay forest, most of the lake is visible. Another of its features now becomes obvious: Jones Lake is an ellipse, actually an ellipse within an ellipse—an elliptical lake occupying a portion of an elliptical bay. Like the sand rims, this shape, this *ovalness*, is a characteristic that all Carolina bays share, but it's noticeable only if you know to look for it—an advantage that early European explorers didn't have.

In his remarkably comprehensive book, *The Mysterious Carolina Bays*, Henry Savage, Jr., outlines the history of European exploration of the bays. John Lawson provided the first written account—a description of his encounter with a Carolina bay during an expedition into the interior of South Carolina in 1700. To cross the bay, Lawson said, his party was forced to "strip stark-naked: and much a-do to save ourselves from drowning in this Fatigue [but] with much a-do got Thro." In his writings, Lawson referred to the bays as "percoarsons."

Later, in 1765, the peripatetic John Bartram and his son William visited two bay lakes in Bladen County—White Lake and Singletary Lake. A few days after that, they encountered Lake Waccamaw. John Bartram described the flora around the lakes and noted their "sandy shoals much like those often found off the Atlantic beaches."

And so it went, with each succeeding observer pointing out yet another feature of the bays. Gradually, geologists came to realize that Carolina bays were not just isolated phenomena but were scattered throughout the Southeast, and by 1930, they recognized that the bays had nine or ten characteristics in common. Three of the more important ones are their oval shape, their nearly unvarying northwest-southeast orientation, and their sand rims raised above the level of the surrounding area.

Since no known geological activity could account for the presence of the bays, the early investigators felt free to speculate—sometimes a little wildly—on their origins. They ascribed the bays' existence to everything from the presence of artesian wells to the dissolving of the underlying clay soil by the acidic peat fill. But with an entire planet to investigate, most geologists still considered Carolina bays minor aberrations until the 1930s, when, for the first time, aerial photographs of the Atlantic coastal plain became available. The photographs showed the incredible number of Carolina bays that existed (at least within the five hundred square miles covered in the initial survey) and just how extraordinarily symmetrical they were. Suddenly, some heavy geological hitters got interested in the bays.

They did not buy the earlier speculations about the bays' origins. Armed with aerial photographs, scientists came up with another theory. A paper appeared in 1933 in the *Journal of Geology*. Its title was "The Carolina 'Bays'—Are They Meteorite Scars?" The new theory—simple, straightforward, and dramatic—was clearly more interesting than artesian wells and dissolved clay. Furthermore, if a certain angle of impact is assumed, a meteorite strike could indeed account for the bays' elliptical shape and for the uniform alignment of their axes. At last, the Carolina bays were at the top of geology's "to do" list.

Jones Lake Trail ends at a campground just west of the picnic area where it began. There are no campers today, so I climb on a picnic table to survey the lake and the bay swamp that surrounds it. I try to visualize a gigantic meteorite storm, the fiery hail that must have poured down here if the extraterrestrial theory of the bays' origin is true. But the only picture that comes to mind is a dark sky with red streaks in it that I once saw on the cover of *Astounding Science Fiction*. In fact, I have no idea what a real meteorite storm would look like, so I decide to move on to Salters Lake; perhaps a different bay will stimulate my imagination.

The walk to Salters Lake begins on a sand road. Though the lake itself is part of Jones Lake State Park, the road to it runs through Bladen Lakes State Forest—a working forest, farmed for timber and used for forestry research projects. One field I pass has recently been cut and replanted with longleaf pines, but other areas are being allowed to reseed naturally. The overall effect is an open, airy landscape, a pleasant change from the bay thickets of Jones Lake. I have read that humans feel most at home in terrain like this because it reminds us of our origins on the open savannas of Africa. In any case, it feels right to me, and the short walk to the lake goes quickly.

Just before reaching Salters Lake, I duck under a gate that leads back into the state park. Warblers zip through the pines, and Carolina jasmine twines its way up the bay trees. Deer and raccoon tracks are everywhere.

First thing I notice about Salters Lake: it's a Jones Lake clone, brown water and white sand ringed by bay forest. In fact, the uniformity of the bays was the main reason geologists became intrigued with them. And as more and more scientists measured and probed the bays, the more common characteristics they found. By 1982, investigators had come up with twenty-nine features common to Carolina bays and had published over 150 papers and books about them. Theorizing about their origin became a staple Ph.D. topic for a generation of geologists.

Despite this attention, the genesis of the bays has remained as shadowy as the forests that grow in them. The meteorite-strike idea explained many of the bays' characteristics, but no meteorite fragments have ever been found in or near a Carolina bay. Today, sentiment vacillates between the meteorite theory and the more complex but less exciting terrestrial theories involving artesian wells, unidirectional winds, and the sandy shores of ancient seas. As expected, my brush with Jones and Salters lakes sheds no further light on this scientific controversy. But on the walk back from Salters Lake, I hear the soft, swishy sound of an evening breeze blowing through the pines. The gentle, steady noise reminds me of one of the more bizarre speculations about the bays.

In 1945, zoologist Chapman Grant, writing in *Scientific Monthly*, proposed my all-time-favorite stranger-than-science-fiction theory about the creation of Carolina bays. He suggested that the bays were the spawning beds of huge schools of now-extinct fish which, like steelhead and shad, migrated annually from the ocean into fresh water to spawn. In the case of the Carolina bays, Grant's theory went, the fresh water came from a great upwelling of artesian springs along the southern Atlantic coast. Once the schools reached the fresh water of the springs, each fish, driven by the ancient and honorable urge to procreate, fanned out its own small bed. The millions of tails swishing in unison cleared the sand from large areas, exposing hard ocean floor. Then the ocean receded, and—voila!—thousands of hard-floored, sand-rimmed Carolina bays were left, pitting the now-dry coastal plain.

Although Grant's theory was almost immediately discredited—how did the spawning beds survive the pounding surf of the receding ocean?—I like it. I like the idea of attaching a wacky proposal like Grant's to the origin of these geological eccentricities. But most of all, I like the thought of all those fish gently swishing their tails in the sand, hollowing out a place for their eggs. Unlike my reaction to the meteorite-strike theory, I can easily visualize the fish, and as the wind swishes through the pines, I almost believe I can hear them.

Before You Go

For More Information —————————————————————
Jones Lake State Park
Route 2, Box 945
Elizabethtown, N.C. 28337
(919) 588-4550

Accommodations —————————————————————————
Elizabethtown–White Lake Chamber of Commerce
P.O. Box 306
Elizabethtown, N.C. 28337
(919) 862-4368

Campgrounds

Twenty campsites sit under the pines west of the picnic area at Jones Lake State Park. The campground is only a few steps from the lake and the loop trail that circles it.

Maps

The map in Jones Lake State Park's free brochure is adequate for these trails.

Special Requirements

A permit is required to enter the Salters Lake section of the park. Permits are free and may be obtained at park headquarters.

Special Precautions

The trail around Jones Lake is boggy in spots; I recommend waterproof boots.

Additional Reading

The Great Cypress Swamps by John V. Dennis, Louisiana State University Press, Baton Rouge, 1988.

The Mysterious Carolina Bays by Henry Savage, Jr., University of South Carolina Press, Columbia, 1982.

A Re-evaluation of the Extraterrestrial Origin of the Carolina Bays by J. Ronald Eyton and Judith I. Parkhurst, Geography Graduate Student Association, University of Illinois, Urbana-Champaign, April 1975.

"Twilight for Junipers" by Lawrence S. Early, *Wildlife in North Carolina* 51, December 1987, 8–15.

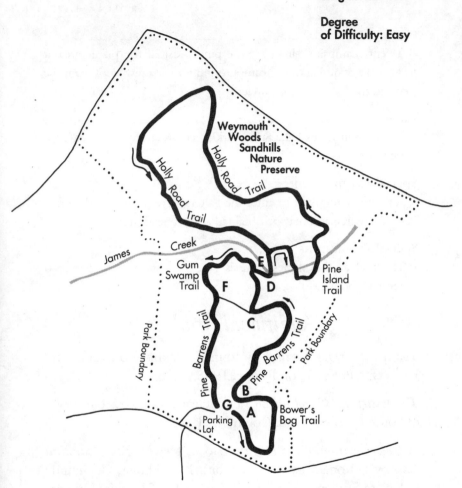

Length: 4.2 miles

Degree
of Difficulty: Easy

Weymouth
Woods
Sandhills
Nature
Preserve

Holly Road Trail

Holly Road Trail

James Creek

Gum
Swamp
Trail

Pine
Island
Trail

F

E

D

C

Pine Barrens Trail

Pine Barrens Trail

Park Boundary

Park Boundary

B

G

A

Parking
Lot

Bower's
Bog Trail

Weymouth Woods Trails

A. Begin Bower's Bog Trail
B. Begin eastern leg of
    Pine Barrens Trail
C. Begin eastern leg of
    Gum Swamp Trail
D. Begin Holly Road loop
    (including Pine Island Trail)
E. End Holly Road loop and
    begin western leg of Gum
    Swamp Trail
F. Begin western leg of
    Pine Barrens Trail

Route and Distances

A. to B.	Bower's Bog Trail	0.5 mi.
B. to C.	Pine Barrens Trail	0.5 mi.
C. to D.	Gum Swamp Trail	0.1 mi.
D. to E.	Holly Road loop	
	(including Pine Island Trail)	2.4 mi.
E. to F.	Gum Swamp Trail	0.2 mi.
F. to G.	Pine Barrens Trail	0.5 mi.
	TOTAL	4.2 mi.

The Sandhills

Weymouth Woods Trails
Weymouth Woods Sandhills Nature Preserve

This walk starts from the parking lot at Weymouth Woods Visitor Center which is located just off Fort Bragg Road, one mile southeast of Southern Pines. Five well-marked trails wind through Weymouth Woods Sandhills Nature Preserve. This generally counterclockwise walk will put you on all of them.

Bower's Bog Trail begins at the visitor center parking lot. After 0.5 mile, it meets the eastern leg of Pine Barrens Trail. Follow Pine Barrens Trail 0.5 mile to Gum Swamp Trail and Holly Road Trail. The Pine Island loop branches off Holly Road Trail, rejoining it 0.5 mile later. After completing the Holly Road loop, return down the western legs of Gum Swamp and Pine Barrens trails. To see the ancient longleaf pines at Weymouth Center, go east from Weymouth Woods on Fort Bragg Road to Connecticut Road, take a left, and proceed west for about a mile. The parking lot for Weymouth Center will be on your right.

As you drive toward Weymouth Woods Sandhills Nature Preserve, the road signs you pass along the way tell you a lot about your destination. They point to towns named Southern Pines, Whispering Pines, and Pinehurst; to golf resorts called Pinewild and Mid-Pines; to the housing developments of Pinebluff Terraces and Pinetree Acres. By the time you reach the preserve, you may guess that you are going to see a pine tree or two there. And you'd be right; you'll see lots of them.

Of course, there are not as many now as there used to be. In pre-Columbian times, pure longleaf-pine forests covered 30 to 60 million acres of the South. The longleaf belt, over a hundred miles wide in places, extended south from the Sandhills of North Carolina down to Florida and west from Alabama almost to the Mississippi River. Today, much of this evergreen river of pines is gone, and in North Carolina, the 425-acre Weymouth Woods is one of the few remnants of this once-extensive forest open to hikers. If you're from the sandy, piney flatlands of the South, Weymouth Woods will feel like home; if you're not, you'll find this quintessentially Southern ecosystem a pleasure to explore.

I begin my walk on a cool, sunshiny day in early November. The leaves on the turkey oaks, the predominant understory, are rust-brown but still cling stubbornly to the branches, contrasting pleasantly with the dark green pines looming above them. The air smells fresh and naturally pine scented; the trail is soft, with longleaf needles and oak leaves cushioning the white sand. The raucous cries of crows ring in the still air.

In the woods, the blackened boles of straight, towering pines stand out against the sand. Although the crowns are healthy and green, fire has charred the trunks of almost every tree from ground level to head height. The fires weren't the result of lightning or accident or arson—uncontrolled fires are dangerous to the surrounding communities and are usually extinguished. Virtually all of the scorched trees visible throughout the preserve are a result of controlled burns started by Mac Goodwin, the superintendent of Weymouth Woods. Deciding when and where and how often to set these fires is an important part of his job, for without the fires there would be no longleaf-pine forest.

Hardwoods tolerate shade better than pines. An understory of oaks can flourish beneath a canopy of pines, but the pines themselves must have direct sunlight to grow. When a mature tree in a pine forest dies, its death allows sunlight to penetrate the canopy. But the sun's rays can reach the seedlings on the forest floor only if there is no understory to shade them. Done right, controlled burns clear out the understory, allowing life-giving sunlight to reach the young pines.

Surface fires do little damage to mature, thick-barked, fire-resistant pines, and even longleaf seedlings withstand fire well. They have stout, well-developed taproots that furnish the young trees the food they need to replenish their fire-damaged needles. Indeed, the longleaf pine is very well adapted to fire, and without it, the pure longleaf forest would be doomed, a subclimax phenomenon, an evergreen ephemeron transforming itself into a hardwood forest.

Natural fires periodically razed the forests of the pine belt for hundreds of thousands of years; the dead needles made good tinder, and lightning provided the spark. One forester has estimated that before man came along, fires swept the Southern pine forests an average of once every two or three years. The legacy of those fires was millions of acres of pure longleaf-pine forest—a legacy we have pretty well used up.

After finishing the short Bower's Bog loop, I head north on Pine Barrens Trail. Here, the understory is more diverse. In addition to the ubiquitous turkey oaks, there are blackjacks, white oaks, and Southern red oaks. Dogwoods show the droopy, dull red leaves of fall, but their tiny white buds are already set, waiting for spring. Small birds flutter in the pines.

To birders, the sexy bird in these parts is the red-cockaded woodpecker, an endangered species. Visitors from all over come here to glimpse members of this fast-disappearing breed. But these birds aren't woodpeckers; they are too small, too numerous, too fluttery. When I finally get my binoculars on one, I see a sparrow-sized bird with a yellow-olive breast and two white bars on its wing. It's a pine warbler, and not rare at all. In fact, in fall and winter, when Yankee warblers migrate south to join the year-round residents, it is one of the more common birds of the Sandhills.

Fifty years ago, this warbler was known as *Dendroica pinus pinus*. Today, it's called *Dendroica pinus*. But even with its shorter name, you don't have to be a Latin scholar to figure out that this is a bird of the pine forests. It prowls the pines' scaly bark, probing for bugs, and is, as one writer says, "very useful in ridding these trees of the various insect pests that injure them." Audubon called these birds pine-creeping warblers, and as they skitter along the branches of the trees near me, I wonder if he didn't get the name right.

This is not virgin forest; most of the pines in the preserve are about a hundred years old. And as I walk north on Holly Road Trail, I see signs of the practice that doomed their forbears. Three-foot wounds, where eighteen-inch-wide sections of bark and sapwood have been stripped away, scar the fire-blackened bases of many trees. Some of them still have small metal gutters affixed to the bottom of the wounds to channel the resin that oozed out of them into tin cups. This resin—bled directly from the trees or extracted by the slow roasting of resin-rich fatwood—made longleaf pines worth more than any other crop that could be grown in the poor soil in which they thrive.

Tar and pitch made from pine resin were exported to England from the colonies as early as 1608 to tar the ropes used in the queen's navy and to seal the hulls and decks of its ships. Resin was also distilled to get turpentine. As a group, these products were called naval stores, and in the days before silicon sealants, nylon ropes, and petroleum distillates, they were big business.

The Sandhills region, with its blanket of virgin pines and its

easy access to the Cape Fear River and the port of Wilmington, made North Carolina an important exporter of naval stores. By 1880, one-third of the world's turpentine came from the state, and North Carolinians had begun to call themselves Tar Heels, an accurate-enough nickname for folks who made their living off the gummy exudate of the longleaf pine.

The regimen was simple: bleed the pines for resin until they weakened or died, cut the trees for timber, then bake the lightwood stumps for yet more tar and turpentine. It was a good, profitable business, and it lasted until the turn of the century. By 1900, the old-growth longleaf-pine forests of North Carolina were gone.

Near the northernmost point of Holly Road Trail, a bulky nest sits high in a longleaf pine. It doesn't look like a gray squirrel's nest—it's too large, and it's in the wrong kind of tree. Grays prefer to nest in hardwoods. More likely, this nest belongs to a fox squirrel, the gray's larger, pine-loving cousin. As I watch the nest, looking for its occupants, the pine warblers become more active, swirling through the trees and brush.

Before I can locate the fox squirrels that I know must be up there, a distinct *tap! tap! tap!* echoes through the pines. It's a woodpecker—a small one, judging from the sound. I stand quietly and wait.

Tap! tap! tap! A small, black-capped, zebra-backed woodpecker is whacking a pine not thirty yards away. I sit down on a log, raise my binoculars, and watch the sexiest bird in the longleaf-pine forest go about its business.

Through some evolutionary quirk, the red-cockaded woodpecker developed a very persnickety nest-building requirement. It will nest and roost only in chambers drilled in large live pines sixty or more years old. Other woodpeckers, even the mighty pileateds, usually chisel their nesting cavities out of the soft, rotting wood of dead trees, but the red-cockaded insists on boring into the hard heartwood of living pines.

Even though some instinct helps them select a high proportion of trees afflicted with red heart, a fungal disease that softens the wood, excavation is tough, and it takes a year or more to chip a nest out of the heartwood. But the hardest part of the woodpeckers' job these days is finding trees old enough to drill in and pine forests large enough to meet their foraging requirements. As old-growth longleaf forests have become increasingly rare, so have red-cockaded woodpeckers.

In 1970, the government added the species to its endangered list. With money available, scientists and academics galloped to the rescue. A plan to save the red-cockaded woodpecker was devised and implemented on federally owned lands. In one national forest, a biologist told me he had seventy-five part-time workers drilling new roosting cavities for the woodpeckers. But red-cockaded woodpecker populations continue to wane. Reversing the course and the side effects of serious environmental damage is a hard—sometimes impossible—job.

The woodpecker in front of me flits up, down, and around the tree so fast that I never see any red or any cockade. Even my field guides, which usually imply that only a birdbrain could miss something as obvious as "rufous shoulders" or a "whitish rump," say that the male's tiny red cockade is hard to see. As I watch, straining to catch that small streak of red, the bird moves to a more distant pine, and then it's gone.

Like the pine warblers that migrate south, Northerners have been streaming into the Sandhills for years. And like the warblers, they usually arrive in the fall and leave in the spring. But every now and then, one of them falls in love with the region and stays. James Boyd was one of those.

His grandfather bought the land now called Weymouth Woods around the turn of the century. Inexplicably, this second-growth patch of Southern pine woods reminded the old gentleman of a forest in England near the town of Weymouth, and he named his purchase after it.

Although the Boyds regularly visited the Sandhills, it wasn't until 1920 that James Boyd moved here permanently. He brought with him some psychic baggage picked up while commanding an ambulance unit in France during World War I, a newfound desire for a literary career, and an estate worth several millions of dollars. He built a fine house just up the road from Weymouth Woods and settled easily into the life of a working country squire, putting the war behind him, writing good stories and well-respected historical novels, and riding to the hounds.

Nineteen years after he died, his wife, Katharine Lamont Boyd, gave Weymouth Woods to the state because, Mac Goodwin says, "she wanted to see the land in the hands of someone who cared." After her death, she left the family mansion and its acreage—now called Weymouth Center—to Sandhills Community College. Later, the state bought much of this land and placed it under the jurisdiction of Weymouth Woods Sandhills Nature Preserve.

There are three-hundred- and four-hundred-year-old longleaf pines at Weymouth Center, and after my walk through the preserve, I drive over to see them. I don't have to look far; the first tree I see is a straight-trunked tower nearly eight feet around. I plop down on the pine straw at its base and try to picture a forest of these giants, but my imagination is small, my vision limited.

A red-tailed hawk rides the wind above me, peering down, and suddenly, as if I, too, were flying, I can see it: mile after mile of soaring pines, a wide, bright green river stretching from North Carolina to Florida, alive with fox squirrels, warblers, and woodpeckers. I know that it's a reified forest, one of the mind, one that will never again exist, but for just a moment I can see it. And it's beautiful.

Before You Go

For More Information ⸻
Weymouth Woods Sandhills Nature Preserve
400 North Fort Bragg Road
Southern Pines, N.C. 28387
(919) 692-2167

Accommodations ⸻
Sandhills Area Chamber of Commerce
P.O. Box 458
Southern Pines, N.C. 28388
(919) 692-3926

Campgrounds ⸻
Camping is not allowed in the preserve. Some nearby campgrounds are listed in the "Accommodations Guide" furnished by the Sandhills Chamber of Commerce.

Maps _____

Trails are very well marked, and the map in the preserve's free brochure is all you'll need.

Additional Reading

James Boyd by David E. Whisnant, Twayne Publishers, New York, 1972.

Life Histories of North American Wood Warblers by Arthur Cleveland Bent, Dover Publications, New York, 1963.

Life Histories of North American Woodpeckers by Arthur Cleveland Bent, Dover Publications, New York, 1964.

Longleaf Pine by W. G. Wahlenberg, Charles Lathrop Pack Foundation, Washington, D.C., 1946.

The Longleaf Pine in Virgin Forest by G. Frederick Schwarz, John Wiley and Sons, New York, 1907.

The Pine Barrens by John McPhee, Farrar, Straus and Giroux, New York, 1968. This book examines the pitch-pine and shortleaf-pine forests of New Jersey, an ecosystem that has much in common with North Carolina's Sandhills.

Length: 8.2 miles

**Degree
of Difficulty: Easy**

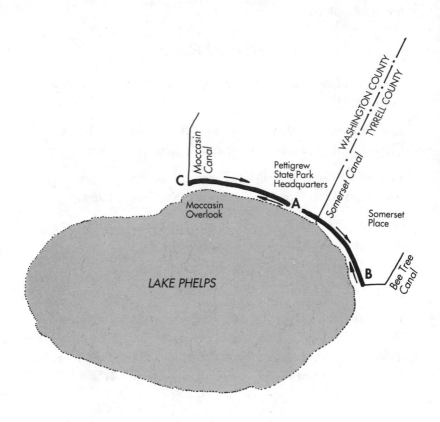

Carriage Drive Trail

A. Pettigrew State Park
   Headquarters and trailhead
   for Carriage Drive Trail
B. Bee Tree Canal Overlook
C. Moccasin Overlook

Route and Distances

A. to B.	Trail to Bee Tree Canal Overlook	1.4 mi.
B. to C.	Bee Tree Canal Overlook to Moccasin Overlook	4.1 mi.
C. to A.	Return to park headquarters	2.7 mi.
	TOTAL	8.2 mi.

A Lowland Forest

Carriage Drive Trail
Pettigrew State Park

Pettigrew State Park is located 7 miles south of Creswell on the border between Washington and Tyrrell counties. There are 2 legs to this walk. The trail to Bee Tree Canal starts at the eastern end of the park campground, curls southeast around Lake Phelps, and ends 1.4 miles later at a short boardwalk which overlooks the lake. The return is by the same route. The second leg starts near the park picnic area and proceeds west for 2.7 miles to Moccasin Overlook. A boardwalk there passes through a fine stand of large bald cypresses and leads to the lake. The return to park headquarters is by the same trail.

The mounted head of a cougar stares down from the wall of the visitor center at Pettigrew State Park, just a few yards from the shores of Lake Phelps. The sign beneath the head says that the last cougar sighting in North Carolina occurred near Lake Phelps in 1930. It goes on to speculate that although the cougar has probably been extirpated in the state, no one knows for sure, and a few may still prowl this area.

It is possible; Lake Phelps lies near the center of the Albemarle Peninsula, the flat and watery thumb of land that divides Albemarle and Pamlico sounds. At one time, the region was as impenetrable and wild as any place in the state. And though European settlers partially tamed it, it's still not 100 percent housebroken.

Much of the great swamp forest that once covered the peninsula is gone, the land diked and drained for logging, then converted to farmland. But remnants of the forest and a wisp of the region's former wildness can be found at Pettigrew State Park. Here, walkers can explore the remains of the old forest and imagine this land as it once was.

With 17,449 acres, Pettigrew is North Carolina's largest state park. But most of it is water; the 16,600-acre Lake Phelps, the second-largest natural lake in the state, lies entirely within its boundaries. The park's visitor facilities are on the northeast shore of the lake, and two carriage trails originate there. The shorter one runs southeast to Bee Tree Canal; the longer one goes west to Moccasin Point. Both trails hug the lake and pass through the fringe of old-growth forest that still rings it.

I start with the trail to Bee Tree Canal. It's a warm, overcast morning, the kind of spring's-just-around-the-corner weather you sometimes get in this part of the country in late February. Huge fields with brown stubbles of corn lie to the left; the swamp forest, a two-hundred-yard-deep border of wildness between trail and lake, is to the right.

Among the roots of the large trees that grow near the trail, five-petaled blue flowers sit atop low-lying masses of dark green leaves. I recognize them immediately; the same flowers line the walk of my own house. They are periwinkles, and they are no more native to this forest than the hybrid tea rose. Wildflower guides refer to them as "European escapes from cultivation," and their presence tells you, as surely as would an old barn or a dilapidated picket fence, that a house once sat nearby.

That house lies a few hundred yards farther down the trail, but it's hardly dilapidated. This is Somerset Place, the mansion built in 1830 by the Collins family—the family that built these carriage trails.

In 1785, Josiah Collins and several other investors from Edenton bought more than one hundred thousand acres of land near Lake Phelps—a region then known as "the Great Alegator Dismal." They imported slaves to drain the swamps, cut the timber, and farm the land. Thirty-one years later, Collins bought out his partners and became sole owner of the properties. After his death, his son, Josiah, Jr., and his grandson, Josiah III, continued to operate the plantation with the not inconsiderable help of over three hundred slaves. The Civil War ended slavery and the Collinses' way of life, and after Josiah III's death in 1863, his widow sold Somerset Place. The United States Department of Agriculture later acquired the house and the land around it. The state leased the property from them and in 1939 created Pettigrew State Park and designated the Collins mansion a historic site.

I've been through Somerset Place, seen the shards of the lives of people we Southerners still like to call the "planter aristocracy." The dining room table is set with fine china, and crystal decanters sit on a nearby sideboard awaiting a servant's hand. The bedrooms and sitting areas are spacious and beautifully furnished. Outside are a cool, thick-walled meat house complete with salted herring and smoked bacon, a blacksmith shop, tree-lined walks, formal gardens, and more.

But no buildings remain to help visitors remember the three hundred people that actually worked the plantation. There are only signs that say a slave hospital once stood here, that the slave quarters used to be there. What did those people, about whom our historical sites tell us so little, think about plantation society, about the "planter aristocracy"? It's a question that the wonderfully restored Somerset Place can't answer—was never designed to answer—so I bypass the house today, happy to walk deeper into the woods.

The path passes into a forest thick with sycamores, black gums, sweet gums, tulip poplars, shagbark hickories, and bald cypresses. No one knows for sure, but the narrow band of forest that borders this shore of Lake Phelps appears to have never been logged. Like Tolstoy's happy families, old forests—whether in the mountains or near the coast—have a similar look. Aside from the big trees, there is a messiness and, at the same time, an unmistakable order about them that's easy to recognize. Huge logs lie scattered about the ground and nourish small plants and mushrooms and young trees; standing trees *look* old, with splintered limbs and lichen-smeared trunks riddled with hollows. Much of what lies along this trail is old-growth forest, probably virgin forest.

Unlike some of the never-cut hardwood coves of the Appalachians, this forest is thick with understory. Farther down the trail, a small thicket of pawpaws, one of the more prominent understory trees, grows beneath the canopies of its towering neighbors. Pawpaws (*Asimina triloba*) are small trees, only thirty feet tall, with large, wrinkled leaves. One reference claims that the name *pawpaw* derives from an Arawakan Indian word for the papaya, an unrelated tropical tree. If true, the mix-up may have occurred because of the similarities between the fruits of the two; both trees produce a yellowish, oblong, edible fruit.

The trail ends at Bee Tree Canal. A short wooden boardwalk leads to the edge of Lake Phelps. The lake is so big that the trees lining the far shore are barely visible. According to Sid Shearin, the park superintendent, this is the cleanest body of water in the state. No springs or streams (or sewer lines or septic tanks) feed into it, and because it is a typical Carolina bay lake, its altitude is slightly higher than most of the ground around it, so it catches little runoff; rainfall alone keeps it filled. It's so clear that on a calm day you can see the bottom. But today, a stiff wind from the west churns the water's surface; the lake appears brown and opaque. I enjoy the breeze for a few minutes, then head back. Along the way, the hammering of woodpeckers reverberates through the swamp.

I stop near park headquarters before beginning the trail to Moccasin Point. A flock of two hundred or so robins has invaded the campground and picnic area. They juke around on the grass, hunting for worms and bugs. It's not uncommon to see large numbers of these birds in a swamp in winter. One ornithologist reported seeing a huge congregation of robins north of here in the Great Dismal Swamp. He estimated there were one million birds in the flock.

Robins frequent swamps because there they can find the berries that make up much of their winter diet. The flock in the Great Dismal, for example, was feeding on gallberries. But robins also migrate in flocks, and since the birds I'm watching are ignoring the berries in the forest, I suspect they may already be moving north. In which case, this flock is minuscule—at least by historic standards. In 1897, an enormous flight of migrating robins was spotted in Florida. Two observers reported seeing the flock. Nobody knows exactly how wide that cloud of robins was, but the two men who saw it were ten miles apart when it passed between them.

After watching the robins for a while, I head toward Moccasin Point. If anything, the trees are even bigger here than along the trail to Bee Tree Canal. Carolina wrens and mockingbirds and red-bellied woodpeckers work the forest below the canopy, but it is the trees that beguile, and after a mile or so, I stop to examine the scaly bark of a particularly imposing sycamore. As usual, its colors, a mottle of browns and whites, remind me of a pinto, the spotted horse of the Western plains.

This tree has an outer layer of gray, fissured bark at its base. Beneath this outer layer lies a thinner layer of brown skin, and below that the smooth white nakedness of the inner bark. As the sycamore grows, its outer bark flakes away in patches, dappling the branches and trunk, giving the tree its unmistakable appearance.

The sheer bulk of these trees is also impressive. This one is over three feet in diameter. Sizable, but a long way from the record; sycamores with diameters greater than five feet can be found near Lake Phelps. And even those are striplings compared to the real giants of the species. Sycamores have the largest trunks of any American hardwood; one monster, measured by François Michaux in Ohio in 1802, was forty-seven feet around. Now, that was a sycamore of substance, a tree I would have *loved* to see.

Just down the trail from the sycamore, a loose pile of white feathers lies scattered across the path. Feather piles, those telltale signs of predator-prey dramas, are common sights to anyone who spends much time in the woods. These are large feathers, indicating that a good-sized bird was attacked here, perhaps an egret or even a chicken that wandered in from a nearby farm. I look for blood, for a half-eaten carcass, but find nothing. The feathers are dry to the touch and look fresh.

Yesterday, while scouting the area, I glimpsed a gray fox trotting along a dirt road not far from this spot. A fox or a house cat could have gotten lucky here earlier this morning. But a bird the size this one must have been would have put up quite a fight against a fox or a cat, and there are no signs of a struggle. Maybe it was the bird's lucky day. Maybe the predator got only a mouthful of feathers.

When I reach Moccasin Point, I eat a sandwich, then lie flat on my back at the end of the boardwalk that leads to the edge of the lake. Waves slurp softly against the pilings. A magnificent stand of Spanish moss–laden bald cypresses grows in the knee-deep water..The silvery moss sways in the wind and twinkles in the midday sun, which has finally penetrated the overcast of the morning. The slow, gentle twisting of the moss is hypnotic and soporific. When I awaken a few minutes later, I feel rested and cheerful, eager for the walk back.

Less than a mile later, I find more feathers, just off the trail, that I must have missed on the walk in. These, too, are large, but they are sooty black instead of white. Again, there is no blood, no carcass, no sign of a struggle. What's attacking the birds of Pettigrew State Park? I haven't the vaguest idea.

The rest of the walk goes quickly. Back at park headquarters, I get into a discussion with Sid Shearin and a couple of botanists who have spent the day in the field collecting plants for a museum. We swap information and stories; I tell them about the feathers along the trail. Without missing a beat, one of the botanists—a young man with a brown mustache, muddy boots, and a friendly smile—launches into a story about a forest-products company that owns extensive tree farms in the Lake Phelps area.

The company recently planted a large number of juniper seedlings, he says. Then the deer population in this part of the country soared, and this winter the hungry deer began feeding on the young trees. Since deer-hunting season was over before the damage was discovered, this presented the company with a problem: how stop the deer from eating the junipers?

According to rumor, the botanist says, the company solved its problem by importing—perfectly legally—two cougars from out west and turning them loose on the company's property, property not far from the park.

"I don't know if the story is true or not," he continues, "but if it is, it was a pretty good idea. Mountain lions love venison."

"And almost any other critters they can catch," the second botanist adds.

"Like birds?" I ask.

"Well, a cougar wouldn't leave much of a mess," the first botanist says. "A few feathers at most. One bite and those birds would be history. Then Mr. Cougar would carry 'em off somewhere to dine in leisure." He pauses and looks toward the lake. "There's still some real rough country around here. It wouldn't surprise me if there was a cougar or two out there." He looks at me and grins. "'Course it's just a rumor," he says.

Before You Go

For More Information
Pettigrew State Park
Route 1, Box 336
Creswell, N.C. 27928
(919) 797-4475

Accommodations
The closest motels are in Plymouth, about 25 miles west of the park. For information, contact
Washington County Chamber of Commerce
701 Washington Street
Plymouth, N.C. 27962
(919) 793-4804

Campgrounds
The park has thirteen campsites, as well as a primitive campground for group camping.

Maps
The map in the park brochure is all you'll need for these well-marked trails.

Points of Interest

Pettigrew State Park is named for General James Johnston Pettigrew, a Confederate War hero who was fatally wounded at Gettysburg. Bonarva, the Pettigrew family's farm, was near the park, and their home—since destroyed—stood next to the Collinses'. A signed footpath off the carriage trail to Bee Tree Canal leads to the family cemetery, a small plot shaded by towering trees.

But human history in the Lake Phelps region goes back much farther than the Pettigrews and the Collinses. A great many Indian artifacts have been found in and around the lake, the most notable of which are ancient canoes. Archaeologists have recovered over 30 dugouts—many still in good condition—from sediment at the bottom of the lake. One is 37 feet long; another is over 4,000 years old.

The canoes were made of cypress logs which had been split and hollowed out by burning. Scientists attribute their well-preserved state to the rot resistance of cypress and to the high acidity of the lake and the lake bed, a condition believed to retard decay.

Two of the dugouts are permanently displayed in the visitor center, and once a year, in September, during Indian Heritage Week, the park trots out a great many more Native American artifacts from its storerooms. During that week only, visitors can see the arrowheads, pottery, and stone gorgets of cultures that existed long before Europeans showed up on these shores.

Additional Reading

Ancient Pots and Dugout Canoes: Indian Life As Revealed By Archeology At Lake Phelps by David Sutton Phelps, Pettigrew State Park, Creswell, N.C., 1989. This short pamphlet is available at no charge from the park.

The Great Dismal: A Carolinian's Swamp Memoir by Bland Simpson, University of North Carolina Press, Chapel Hill, 1990.

Life Histories of North American Thrushes, Kinglets, and Their Allies by Arthur Cleveland Bent, Dover Publications, New

York, 1964. Originally published in 1949 as Smithsonian Institution United States National Museum *Bulletin 196.*

A Natural History of Trees of Eastern and Central North America by Donald Culross Peattie, Houghton Mifflin Company, Boston, 1948.

Somerset Homecoming by Dorothy Spruill Redford with Michael Dorso, Doubleday, New York, 1988. This book is the story of a reunion of the descendants of slaves who worked at Somerset Plantation. It gives some of the history that I felt was lacking at the historical site.

Wildflowers of the Shenandoah Valley and Blue Ridge Mountains by Oscar W. Gupton and Fred C. Swope, University Press of Virginia, Charlottesville, 1979.

Length: 6.7 miles

**Degree
of Difficulty: Easy**

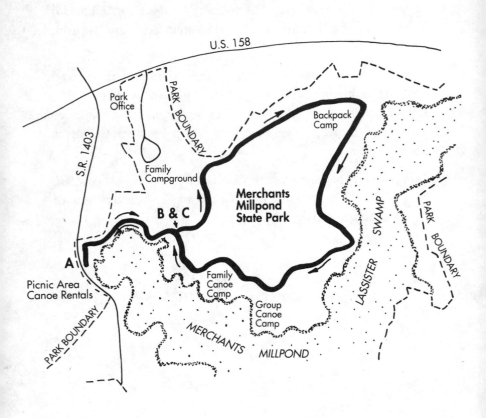

U.S. 158

Park
Office

S.R. 1403

PARK BOUNDARY

Family
Campground

B & C

A

Picnic Area
Canoe Rentals

PARK BOUNDARY

Backpack
Camp

**Merchants
Millpond
State Park**

Family
Canoe
Camp

Group
Canoe
Camp

LASSISTER SWAMP

PARK BOUNDARY

MERCHANTS

MILLPOND

Lassister Swamp Trail

A.   Trailhead
B., C. Begin and end loop trail

Route and Distances

A. to B.   0.8 mi.
B. to C.   5.1 mi.
C. to A.   0.8 mi.

TOTAL 6.7 mi.

A Flooded Forest

Lassiter Swamp Trail
Merchants Millpond State Park

From U.S. 158, take State Road 1403 to
Merchants Millpond State Park's picnic
and canoe-rental area. The walk starts just
north of the bridge over Bennetts Creek.
The well-marked trail first skirts the edge
of the millpond and at 0.8 mile intersects
with the loop trail. It then proceeds
clockwise through an upland forest of
beech, oak, sweet gum, and loblolly pine.
At the loop's easternmost extent, the path
turns south and parallels the western edge
of Lassiter Swamp. After 4 miles, the trail
turns west and leads back to the millpond.

Martha, an old friend and amateur naturalist from Chicago, walked this trail with me. We went in early May, and I'd like to think that the angry red welts which appeared a few days later on our legs and in other, more sensitive areas were not due to my bull-headedness, but stemmed rather from an inexorable chain of events that started when the last gray wolf in North Carolina was killed in 1887.

Not that wiping out wolves was unique to North Carolina; Virginia paid a bounty for wolf heads as early as 1632. In fact, the elimination of predators has been an official policy of our government for most of its history. It was a policy supported by most naturalists in the early years of this century, including a young graduate of Yale's School of Forestry, an Iowan named Aldo Leopold.

In his book, *Speaking of Nature*, Paul Brooks quotes Leopold: "It is going to take patience and money to catch the last wolf or lion in New Mexico, but the last one must be caught before the job can be called fully successful." Later, Leopold wrote *A Sand County Almanac*, a book which includes an impassioned plea for wilderness areas and calls for the protection of predators within those areas. The event that changed his mind has become known as "the lesson of the Kaibab."

Kaibab National Forest is in Arizona, near the north rim of the Grand Canyon. To protect the deer and sheep and cattle that grazed there in the 1920s, the United States Forest Service decided to eliminate wolves and other large predators from the Kaibab. The effort was successful, and after the predators were gone, Leopold described the result:

> *I have watched the face of many a newly wolfless mountain, and seen the south-facing slopes wrinkle with a maze of new deer trails. I have seen every edible bush and seedling browsed, first to anaemic desuetude, and then to death. I have seen every edible tree defoliated to the height of a saddle-horn. Such a mountain looks as if someone had given God a new pruning shears and forbidden Him all other exercise. In the end the starved bones of the hoped-for deer herd, dead of its own too-much, bleach with the bones of the dead sage, or moulder under the high-lined junipers.*

Unfortunately, the lesson of the Kaibab—the overpopulation

and decline of a species due to disease and starvation when man eliminates its natural predators—has been a lesson frequently forgotten. The dreary, predictable cycle that Leopold witnessed has repeated itself time and again as man has replaced nature as the ultimate decider of which animals will live and which will die. It was a lesson that came to mind as Martha and I walked the well-maintained loop trail at Merchants Millpond State Park. Even at midday, we twice encountered groups of deer browsing within a hundred yards of the trail, and I suspect we passed many more that we didn't see. There are a lot of deer in the park, and if it's not overpopulated now, it's close to it.

We started our walk at the park's picnic area, near the dam that created the millpond. According to one historian, Bennetts Creek was first dammed by Kinchen (or Kincken) Norfleet in 1811. Another historian states, equally unambiguously, that it was Rufus Williams in 1857. No matter. The pond has been here awhile, and it's aged well. Much of it is covered with a patina of small aquatic plants, some of which are rare and endangered. But unless you're a research biologist, the first thing you'll notice about the pond is the trees.

Tall tupelo gums and bald cypresses grow in its shallow waters, and as you walk the first three-quarters of a mile of this trail—the part that skirts the millpond—you'll get a good look at them. The trees have swollen bases and towering trunks and canopies dripping with Spanish moss. They rise out of the water and the early-morning mist, spooky and calm on a windless day, imparting a sense of timelessness that makes you forget that the pond is man-made.

As you walk, you'll trip over cypress knees, smooth and cone-shaped, projecting upward from the trees' roots. And you'll likely wonder what their purpose is. The answer has changed through the years, and in a reversal of the normal course of scientific knowledge, the longer scientists have studied these queer knobs, the less certain they have become of their function.

In the 1950s, when life and science were simpler, botanists believed—no, *knew*—that the function of cypress knees was to absorb oxygen from the air and circulate it to the submerged roots of the trees. But in the questioning sixties, a researcher at Duke showed that no oxygen was passed between knees and roots. Botanists then speculated that the purpose of the knees was to stabilize the trees, to hold the roots down in the soft pond muck where cypresses usually grow. By the time the doubting seventies rolled around, scientists admitted that they really didn't know why cypresses had knees. And in the eighties, the Audubon Society's *Field Guide to North American Trees* described cypress knees but did not discuss their function.

This "the-more-you-learn-the-less-you-know" experience is not uncommon in natural history. Good science requires experimental evidence, and good experiments require scientists to control all environmental variables. That's hard to do when you're in the field dealing with wolves and deer and hundred-year-old cypresses.

After the first mile, the cypresses disappear, and the trail passes into a wood of beeches, oaks, and pines. Much of this is old-growth forest with little understory, more like a painting from the Hudson River school than the shrubby, vine-entangled jungles that sometimes pass for forests in the South.

Where there were openings in the canopy, bright cylinders of sunlight spotlighted huge, glistening spider webs on the forest

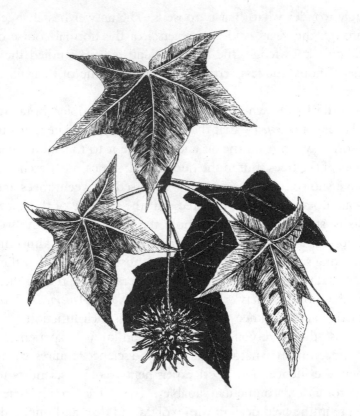

floor. A mature forest must constantly regenerate itself, but—as in the Kaibab—the deer had mowed down the saplings that should have been growing in the sun-drenched spots, leaving the forest floor to spiders and, as we discovered later, to other, more troublesome arachnids.

There were a lot of ups and downs on this part of the walk, short climbs up gentle slopes, a stroll along a ridge, then a descent again. Large beeches dominate the slopes, while pines and oaks monopolize the uplands. There is also enough wildlife to keep you alert. Besides deer, we saw sparrows, jays, warblers, and crows. Some birds we only heard, and one was particularly easy to identify; the brain-rattling *thonk, thonk, thonk* of pileated woodpeckers resounded through the forest for much of our walk.

Pileateds are crow-sized woodpeckers with flaming red crests—living Woody Woodpeckers. They're big enough that when they whack away at a tree, the sound can be heard throughout the forest. And every time I hear one, I wonder, Is it really a pileated? Could it be its first cousin? Could it be an ivory bill?

This is romantic nonsense, of course. The ivory-billed wood-pecker, slightly larger than the pileated, is almost certainly extinct in the United States. And even if it isn't, Roger Tory Peterson and other professional birders have spent years scouring the country for one. The chance of my finding an ivory bill when they haven't is laughable.

But I've been lucky before: I once spotted a rare Florida panther crossing a road in southern Florida. When I called Fish and Game to report it, I talked to a biologist who had spent eleven years tracking panthers. In that entire time, he said, he had never seen one. He'd seen their tracks, their scat, but never the real thing. *Was I sure?*

After I described the animal, he agreed that it probably had been a Florida panther. Luck is still a part of the natural world, so I'll continue to keep an eye open for the unlikely—for ivory bills and panthers and gray wolves.

About halfway around the loop, the trail veers south and parallels Lassiter Swamp. In the swamp's deepest recesses, well away from the trail and accessible only by canoe, is a never-cut stand of bald cypresses. These are huge trees, I'm told, eight feet in diameter and, according to one expert, over one thousand years old. That means they were standing at the time of the Norman Conquest and were already several hundred years old when Pope Alexander III laid the foundation stone for Notre Dame de Paris.

Just beyond the backpack camp located on the western edge of Lassiter Swamp, we paused to watch dragonflies and stare in the direction of those ancient trees. Gums and cypresses grow in the swamp, as they do in the millpond, and their reflections in the still water give the same feeling of hushed, soaring antiquity that strikes one in a cathedral. There's a sense of permanence about places like this, a permanence that imparts a healthy sense of one's own transience. This is valuable terrain—irreplaceable, in fact. And as is often the case with natural areas, the fight for its preservation started not in the councils of government or the committees of academia but with an individual, one person acting alone. In this case, that person was Allan B. Coleman of Moyock, North Carolina.

Coleman, a land developer, acquired the millpond, which lies in Gates County, in the early sixties. His intent was to develop the land around it. At that time, he said, the pond was "overfished, overshot, and in a state of total destruction." He began visiting there regularly. The more he saw of the pond, the more he saw a need to protect it. "I finally got to the point where I just couldn't develop it," Coleman said. He gave the property to his son, who offered to donate it to the state.

The idea of a swamp park appealed to state officials, but some of them opposed the site, favoring instead a park in the Great Dismal Swamp. "Nobody wanted the park here," Coleman said. "Not the state, not the fishermen, not the duck hunters, and certainly not the powers that be in Gates County." That the last group opposed the park surprised me; having read a history of the county, I figured that the locals were a fair-minded bunch, the sort of people that usually favor state parks.

In 1976, the Gates County Arts Council published its *History of Gates County*. The book was the work of several writers, and their lead-off man was Isaac Samuel Harrell. Harrell was a native of Gates County who earned a Ph.D. in history from the University of Pennsylvania and later taught at New York University. But he wrote the history of his home county while he was still a student at Trinity College (now Duke University). And he wrote it with a poison pen; somehow, Isaac Harrell had come to detest his birthplace. One example of his distaste shows up in the conclusion of his work: "As was said in the beginning, this account of Gates County has not been written because of any great achievements that its citizens have accomplished. There have been no great men or great movements in Gates that have stirred state and nation; it has been a mediocre county and its people have been a mediocre people."

Folks that will publish a document like that about themselves get my respect. That's why I was surprised to hear that the "powers that be" had resisted the park. When I read Harrell's history more carefully, I found a clue. In the body of the text, he tells readers that nothing much ever happened in Gates County because "everyone was satisfied with things as they were." Apparently, Harrell got that part right; despite the fact that many Gates Countians originally opposed it, Coleman said, "now that the park's here, they love it."

So do a lot of other creatures; over 190 bird species have been spotted in the 2,918-acre park since it was created in 1973.

Beaver, mink, and otter also live here. But as Martha and I walked along the edge of Lassiter Swamp, the signs we noticed weren't left by any animal featured in the park's brochures—they were left by bears. The bark had been scraped off above head height on two trees near the trail, and claw marks were clearly visible. Floyd Williams, the chief ranger at the park, believes the bears were just passing through, strays from the Great Dismal. But permanent or transient, the bears' presence added to the sense of wilderness we felt. At least it did for me. Martha's reaction was different: she picked up the pace.

I didn't find any reason to hurry until we turned west to begin the final leg of the walk. That's when the predators jumped us, and our attackers were far more fearsome than bears. During the last two miles, Martha and I constantly brushed ticks off every part of our bodies and clothing. They were behind every bush and under every leaf. They were on trees and logs, and they infested every stump. They ambushed us while we walked and attacked en masse if we sat down. We pulled off the big ones, but the small ones, tiny eight-legged devils called seed ticks, were impossible to find—until the welts appeared a few days later.

Back at park headquarters after the walk, I asked Floyd Williams about the huge number of ticks in the park. "Warm bodies," he said. "We have a lot of warm-blooded animals here, mainly deer. Too many deer, in fact. And not just here, all over the county. More deer mean more ticks."

"Overpopulated," I said. "Just like the Kaibab. What this park needs is predators. Maybe some wolves. They'd hold down the deer."

"I guess so," he said. "We don't have a Kaibab on our hands, but a few wolves might help. Either that or people that can read. Didn't you see our sign?"

It was a rhetorical question. The sign, a stern warning informing hikers of the infestation of ticks along the trail, was big and had been posted prominently at the trailhead. *Nobody* could have missed it, but over Martha's objections, I had insisted on going ahead with our walk.

"We're proud of our trail," Floyd continued. "But it's not smart to walk it this time of year. Why did you?"

"Bullheaded?" I speculated.

Floyd grinned and nodded.

And I guess he was right. But I still think a wolf or two might have made a difference.

Before You Go

For More Information ——————————————————
Merchants Millpond State Park
Route 1, Box 141-A
Gatesville, N.C. 27938
(919) 357-1191

Accommodations ——————————————————
The nearest accommodations are in Edenton, about 25 miles south of the park. For information, contact
Edenton-Chowan Chamber of Commerce
P.O. Box 245
Edenton, N.C. 27932
(919) 482-3400

Campgrounds

Twenty family campsites are located south of the park's main entrance on U.S. 158. Merchants Millpond also has a few back-country campsites for canoeists and backpackers.

Maps

The park brochure contains an excellent map—all you will need for this well-marked trail.

Special Precautions

Ticks are no joke; they are major carriers of disease. Both Rocky Mountain spotted fever and Lyme disease occur in North Carolina. The park is generally free of ticks between early October and the middle of April, so plan your walk for the cool months. To make sure the trail is tick-free, call the park for an up-to-the-minute report before you go.

Points of Interest

The Great Dismal Swamp is northeast of Merchants Millpond State Park. Although most of it is in Virginia, a visitor center for the Dismal Swamp Canal (a national historic landmark) is in North Carolina, off U.S. 17 near South Mills. Information and maps are available there.

In November 1986, the United States Fish and Wildlife Service released four pairs of red wolves into the wild at the Alligator River National Wildlife Refuge. It's too early to tell if this attempt to reestablish wolves in North Carolina will succeed. For up-to-date information, contact the refuge at P.O. Box 1969, Manteo, N.C. 27954.

Additional Reading

Forgotten Gates: The Historical Architecture of a Rural North Carolina County by Thomas R. Butchko, Gates County Historical Society, Gatesville, N.C., 1991.

"A Fragile Wilderness" by Lou Clemmons, *Tar Heel* 7, July/August 1979, 34–35.

"Gates County to 1860" by Isaac S. Harrell, in *History of Gates County*, 1–39, Gates County Arts Council, Gatesville, N.C., 1976.

"Lovely, Beautiful, Merchants Millpond" by Nancy Patterson, *New East* 4, January/February 1976, 22–25.

"Merchants Millpond State Park, 4000 B.C.–1950 A.D., A Brief History of Its Land and People" by Mary Belden. This unpublished work is available at the park office.

A Sand County Almanac by Aldo Leopold, Oxford University Press, New York, 1949.

Speaking for Nature by Paul Brooks, Sierra Club Books, San Francisco, 1980.

Cape Hatteras Lighthouse

THE BARRIER ISLANDS

*Whales are very numerous, on
the Coast of North Carolina,
from which they make Oil, Bone,
etc. to the great Advantage of
those inhabiting the Sand-Banks,
along the Ocean, where these
Whales come ashore.*

John Lawson, 1709

Length: 4.8 miles

**Degree
of Difficulty: Easy**

Hwy. 12

Oregon   Inlet

Pea Island National Wildlife Refuge

ATLANTIC

OCEAN

Hwy. 12

E

D

Pamlico
Sound

North
Pond

North
Pond
Trail

A

C   B

North Pond Trail

A. Comfort station and
    parking lot
B. First observation tower
C. Second observation tower
D. Third observation tower
E. Path from Highway 12 to beach

Route and Distances

A. to D.	North Pond Trail	2.8 mi.
D. to E.	Path to beach	0.1 mi.
E. to A.	Return on beach	1.9 mi.
	TOTAL	4.8 mi.

Birds and Beaches

North Pond Trail
Pea Island National Wildlife Refuge

North Pond Trail starts at a comfort station and parking lot on N.C. 12, 4 miles south of Oregon Inlet. The trail leads south and west for about 100 yards to an observation tower. From there, it goes west to a second tower, then north, around the western edge of the impoundment, to a third tower. To return by way of the beach, proceed north on the shoulder of N.C. 12 for 200 yards to a path through the dunes that leads to the ocean. Walk south on the beach for 2 miles to a second trail through the dunes that leads back to the parking lot. No trails on this walk are marked, but Pea Island is so narrow and so flat that it is hard to get lost.

*I*n 1937, Congress designated thirteen miles of North Carolina's Outer Banks as Pea Island National Wildlife Refuge. The northern boundary is Oregon Inlet, and the refuge extends south almost to the town of Rodanthe. The skinny tract includes 5,915 acres of land and 25,700 acres of Pamlico Sound. Pea Island was named for the wild dune peas which grow along the beaches in this area, but the name of the refuge is a bit misleading, since Pea Island no longer exists. Like the rest of the Outer Banks, this section of Hatteras

Island is a work in progress, an ever-changing form created by the easy interchange of sand and sea. This geographic fluidity is worrisome to us stability-seeking, property-owning humans, but it doesn't seem to bother the wildlife. The refuge is usually packed with birds, and in January, waterfowl are especially abundant and varied.

Before I get out of the parking lot, a high-flying flock of ducks, perhaps a hundred birds, cruises over North Pond. The morning is cold and overcast, and the air smells of rain. The birds are flying east, toward the ocean. I've read that the waterfowl guides of yesteryear, men who spent almost every day of the long hunting seasons of that era on the water, could identify any duck they could see, no matter how far away it was. It's a knack I don't have, and though I assume these are diving ducks heading to sea to feed, they are too far away for me to identify. Birders call birds too distant to name "LBJs"—Little Brown Jobs—and in my notes for the day, it is a term I will use time and again.

The trail begins on a sidewalk that runs for a hundred yards or so under a canopy of live oaks, bayberries, and wax myrtles that have been sculpted into odd, lopsided shapes by the heavy sea winds. Beyond the sidewalk, a rabbit skips across the dirt trail that circles North Pond, an impoundment built by the Civilian Conservation Corps in the late 1930s. Five bobwhites flush from the grass and flutter a few feet before vanishing into the low brush that lies between trail and pond. Large numbers of tundra swans and ducks float serenely on the smooth, black surface of the pond. The trail is flat, the walking easy.

At the low tower near the southwestern edge of the impoundment, a dozen or so large white birds flash across the sky.

These are the creatures for which this refuge is famous, and their black wing tips give them away. They are snow geese, moving fast and flying low.

Even in the coldest winters, North Carolina is about as far south as these geese go, and only a few thousand of them make it to Pea Island. Those that do get here are bushed; they have flown almost three thousand miles by the time they arrive.

The snow geese that winter at Pea Island nest in Canada's Northwest Territories, up around Ellesmere Island, only eight hundred miles from the North Pole. The name *snow goose* fits these birds well, recalling both their far-northern nesting areas and their nearly all-white plumage. However, another name for the species appears to be a misnomer: they are sometimes called blue geese.

The name comes from dark-phase snow geese—brown birds with white heads and a hint of blue on their wing coverts. Except for the birds' color, most ornithologists believe that dark- and white-phase snow geese are indistinguishable. Blue geese usually migrate down the Pacific and mid-continent flyways, but occasionally a few get off course. Refuge employees have spotted them at Pea Island mingling happily with white-phase geese in integrated flocks.

I climb the tower to scan the impoundment. It is filled with birds—feeding, swimming, preening waterfowl—most of them too far away to identify. I can make out the Canadas, swans, and snow geese, but everything else is an LBJ. Closer to shore, the viewing is better. Great blue herons stalk the shallows, and eight white ibises shuffle around a small island. Over the marsh that lies to the west of the pond, a line of pelicans cruises by, alternating powerful wingbeats with short, silky glides. A large brown animal too big to be a muskrat swims lazily in the dark water. It is a nutria, an import from Argentina, where it is known as the coypu.

In his book, *The Alien Animals*, George Laycock says that these rodents were imported into Louisiana in 1938, about the time this impoundment was being built. Despite periods of intensive trapping for their fur, the nutria multiplied and spread throughout the Southeast. Since then, they've extended their range even farther; the last one I saw was sitting by a pond not unlike this one in the Camargue, a marshy region in southern France. It was eating dog food out of a shiny aluminum pie pan.

Like white-tailed deer, coyotes, and a few other species, nutria thrive in close contact with humans. But because of the damage they do to crops and to the dikes and levees in which they dig their burrows, they are considered pests by farmers. They are awkward, ugly creatures on land, and it's hard to find a good word written about them. But they are graceful swimmers, and I watch the one below the tower for a long time before I walk on.

The trail around the western edge of the impoundment is an old Jeep road, partially grown over. A low line of grass-covered, man-made hillocks (probably created when the impoundment was scooped out) lies to the west of the trail. Flocks of geese and swans and ducks regularly sweep over these hillocks, returning to the pond after an early breakfast in the fields of nearby farms. Seaside sparrows and yellow-rumped warblers flit through the low bushes that grow at the base of the hills, and several small ducks with heads that look too large for their bodies swim on the pond near the shore.

I've seen several hundred ducks today and have yet to identify a single one. But these are closer and unmistakable. They are bufflehead, three black-and-white beauties. I consider a career as a waterfowl guide, but discard the notion quickly when a small flock of ducks explodes from the water not twenty feet away. They fly to the center of the impoundment, giving me only a hind-end view. I scratch my head and make a note: four LBJs.

This is a birders' walk, and by the time I reach the third observation tower, I've seen hundreds of birds and identified a dozen or so species, from kingfishers to marsh hawks to American widgeon. And my tally barely scratches the surface. According to the refuge's brochure, 265 species regularly visit Pea Island, and another 50 show up occasionally. In the spring, shorebirds nest here, and in the fall, raptors congregate in the area before moving farther south. According to Bonnie Strawser, a wildlife specialist at the refuge, an ornithology class from North Carolina State University saw twenty-six peregrine falcons here in a single day.

But Pea Island is more than marshland and impoundments,

and its other face lies just east of N.C. 12. So after finishing North Pond Trail, I walk a few hundred yards north on the highway to a path through the dunes.

In this part of the country, winter beaches bear little resemblance to the soft shores of summer. They have an entirely different look to them, an entirely different *feel*. The light is paler, more subdued. The waves are bigger and more thunderous and somehow menacing, as if the sea wants to reach out and grab you and suck you into its chill, dark maw. The beaches are cold, windy, and littered with shells and tidal wrack. And of course, they are deserted, not a soul as far as the eye can see. There is a wildness about winter beaches, something in the air, something that never fails to excite me. I love places like this.

Herring gulls and ring-bills line the shore. These birds will attack you for food in the summer, but they won't let me within fifty feet of them now, so I concentrate on the shells scattered along the beach. They are bigger and heavier than the shells of summer: thick surf clams and big, shiny scallops, oysters, cockles, and arks. I dig a knobbed whelk out of the sand.

Whelk shells are common on the beaches of North Carolina, but there seem to be fewer of them these days, perhaps because the beaches are more crowded—at least in summer—and the shells are found more quickly by beachcombers. This one is good-sized, maybe seven inches long. The creature that once lived in it has been dead for quite a while, and the aperture—bright orange on fresh shells—has faded to dull brown.

Whelks are snails, members of the mollusk phylum, and like all snails, they are classified as gastropods. Also like other snails, they have a single, muscular foot. Their gills and their size differentiate them from common garden snails—as do their eating habits.

Whelks are carnivorous, cheerfully devouring both live prey and carrion. Like many of us, they love clams. But extracting those sweet morsels from their shells, as anyone who has ever tried to open an uncooked clam will confirm, can be a little troublesome. Consider the whelk's problem, then; think about prying a clam from its shell with no hands, and only one foot.

The whelk does it by wedging the edge of its shell between the clam's two shells to force them open. The whelk then inserts its proboscis and uses its fine-toothed radulae to rasp the unfortunate clam into bite-sized bits. It's a messy process, one that few people have seen or would want to.

Luckily (or unluckily, depending on how you feel about such things), I am one of those few. Years ago, I found a live whelk in the surf. It had attached itself to a good-sized cockle. The cockle's top shell had been crushed (presumably by the whelk), and what that whelk was doing to that cockle was not a pretty sight.

About a mile down the beach, the signs of the severe northeaster that battered the Outer Banks earlier this winter become obvious. During that storm, an overwash flattened many of the dunes, and those left have been undercut and are half gone, leaving crumbling, nearly vertical sand cliffs to face the ocean. The waves have exposed huge chunks of asphalt, which litter the beach like black icebergs in a sea of white sand. Refuge officials believe that the asphalt chunks are the remains of an old highway which fell into disuse when it was overwashed years ago. Clearly, overwashes are nothing new here; they have occurred regularly along this coast since the first sand bar pushed itself above the ocean's surface. But the question people keep asking is, What can be done to stop them?

Driving to the refuge this morning, I saw head-high mounds of sand lining both sides of sections of N.C. 12, the thin, two-lane strand of asphalt that connects Cape Hatteras to Nags Head, Manteo, and the rest of the world. The sand had been dumped on the highway by the same overwash that exposed the remains of the old road. The state had then bulldozed the sand into temporary dunes alongside the highway to try to protect it from the next storm. Threats to N.C. 12 are big news in this part of the country, and in the paper just this morning, local residents—especially those south of Oregon Inlet—were howling for the state to do more. They were concerned because another overwash might severely damage N.C. 12 or—worse yet—create a new inlet that would cut them off from the mainland and their lifeblood, the tourist trade that rolls down the highway in the summer.

They have good reason to worry; at one time, there *was* another inlet in this vicinity. New Inlet, as it was called, was located just a few miles south of this year's washout. It separated Pea Island from Hatteras Island. In his history of the Outer Banks, David Stick details the inlet's openings and closings from the time it first appeared on a map in 1738. It opened for the last time during the hurricanes of 1933 and closed again shortly after that. But names die slowly, and when the refuge was created four years later, it was named after Pea Island—an island that no longer existed.

These days, the sea appears determined to correct that no-menclatural error—appears determined to re-create Pea Island despite the best efforts of the state of North Carolina. I sympa-thize with the residents for whom this would create substantial hardships, and I believe the state will undertake projects to help them. These projects may produce short-term victories, but I've got my doubts about the state's chances for ultimate success. In games like this, as many naturalists have observed, nature bats last.

Before You Go

For More Information
Pea Island National Wildlife Refuge
P.O. Box 150
Rodanthe, N.C. 27968
(919) 987-2394
   The refuge also has an office in Manteo. For information, write or call
Pea Island National Wildlife Refuge
P.O. Box 1969
Manteo, N.C. 27954
(919) 473-1131

Accommodations
   Motels are available in Manteo and Nags Head. For information, contact
Dare County Tourist Bureau
P.O. Box 399
Manteo, N.C. 27954
(919) 473-2138

Outer Banks Chamber of Commerce
P.O. Box 1757
Kill Devil Hills, N.C. 27948
(919) 441-8144

Campgrounds _____

Pea Island is surrounded by Cape Hatteras National Seashore. There are five campgrounds in the seashore. One of them, Oregon Inlet Campground, is just a few miles north of North Pond. The campgrounds are open only during the summer season. For more information, contact

Cape Hatteras National Seashore
Route 1, Box 675
Manteo, N.C. 27954
(919) 473-2111

Maps _____

The map in the free brochure that the refuge hands out to visitors is adequate for this walk.

Additional Reading

The Alien Animals by George Laycock, Natural History Press, Garden City, N.Y., 1966.

Ducks, Geese and Swans of North America by Frank C. Bellrose, Stackpole Books, Harrisburg, Pa., 1976.

The Outer Banks of North Carolina by David Stick, University of North Carolina Press, Chapel Hill, 1958.

The Wild Edge: Life and Lore of the Great Atlantic Beaches, 2d ed., by Philip Kopper, Globe Pequot Press, Chester, Conn., 1991.

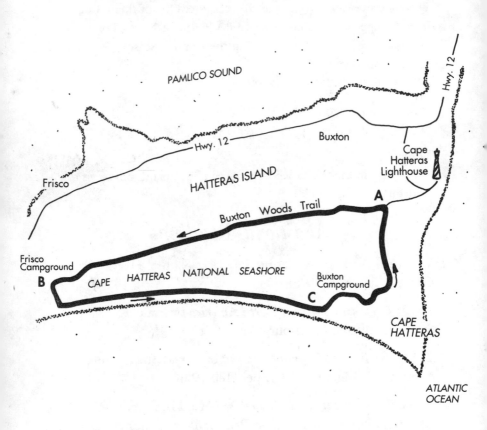

Length: 9 miles

Degree
of Difficulty: Moderate

PAMLICO SOUND

Hwy. 12

Buxton

Cape
Hatteras
Lighthouse

Frisco

HATTERAS ISLAND

A

Buxton Woods Trail

Frisco
Campground

B

CAPE   HATTERAS   NATIONAL   SEASHORE

Buxton
Campground

C

CAPE
HATTERAS

ATLANTIC
OCEAN

Buxton Woods Trail

A.   Trailhead for Buxton Woods Trail
B.   Frisco Campground
C.   Sand road leading from the beach
     to Buxton Campground

Route and Distances

A. to B.	Buxton Woods Trail	3.7 mi.
B. to C.	Beach walk	3.4 mi.
C. to A.	Return to trailhead via Buxton Campground	1.9 mi.
	TOTAL	9.0 mi.

The Maritime Forest

Buxton Woods Trail
Cape Hatteras National Seashore

The walk begins 0.5 mile from the Cape Hatteras Lighthouse. To find the trailhead, proceed south from the lighthouse toward Buxton Campground. Near the trailer dumping station, a sand road leads west into the forest. The sign at the gate reads "North Carolina Trail Systems— Cape Hatteras Beach Trail." The trail forks after 1.5 miles. Take the right fork (the trail with a cable across it) and continue west until you reach Frisco Campground, 3.7 miles from the trailhead. From the campground, head south on the long wooden boardwalk to the shore, then walk east on the beach. After another 3.4 miles, a sand road leads northeast from the beach to Buxton Campground. Since this road is unmarked—and is one of many that crisscross this part of Hatteras Island—you should use a map to determine the line between shore and lighthouse that intersects the campground. As you walk, use your map to guess at the point where you should angle off the beach and head toward the lighthouse. Follow the roads—with an occasional glance at the lighthouse to keep you on course—to the campground. From there, it is 1 mile back to the trailhead.

As anyone who lives on the Outer Banks or visits often can tell you, change is the only constant in these islands. Inlets come and go, boat channels shift, and sand bars appear or disappear overnight. You can walk to spots today that you needed a boat to reach last year, and the sand spit you stood on to cast for bluefish in October has vanished by May. Just keeping up with the topography of these islands is hard, and predicting their future contours is like predicting the flight of a butterfly—you might get the general direction right, but you're going to miss some dips and turns along the way.

The most famous landmark on the Outer Banks is a case in point. In *The Beaches Are Moving*, Wallace Kaufman and Orrin H. Pilkey, Jr., predict

that "if the new policy [letting nature take its course] works, the famous Cape Hatteras Lighthouse will fall into the Atlantic Ocean before 1985." But even though the National Park Service has done little to intervene in the lighthouse's behalf, the structure was still standing in 1992—seven years after its predicted topple into the Atlantic—and the beacon atop the familiar black-and-white spiral continued to punctuate the night as regularly as it did in 1870 when it was built.

It is not clear exactly when the first few grains of sand that would become Cape Hatteras were pushed above the surface of the Atlantic, but it was probably about three to four thousand years ago. The last Ice Age was past, and the planet was warming rapidly. The seas were rising as meltwater from the glaciers and from the heavy snows of the Ice Age poured into the oceans, bringing huge quantities of gravel and sand with it. Suddenly, for reasons unknown, the climate began to cool. The rise in sea level slowed, and the sand from the rivers began to accumulate faster than the water rose. The Outer Banks began to emerge from the sea.

Dunes formed and grass seeds were deposited upon them by seabirds and wind. The grasses stabilized the dunes, and even in the face of a slowly rising sea, the islands grew. The nascent dunes of Cape Hatteras were pounded by sand-heavy waves and caressed by south-flowing currents, so the island grew southward and westward. Dunes that once guarded its Atlantic shore were left behind as new dunes formed to the south. The newer dunes sheltered the older ones from the worst of the sea winds and salt spray. Overwashes—shallow rivers of deadly, storm-driven salt water that periodically washed over the new island—became less frequent as the island grew larger and finally stopped altogether. Rainwater collected in the sand and, because of its lower density, floated on the salt-water-soaked sand beneath it. On the far side of the island, among the sea oats near the sound, a red cedar sprouted. The forest that was to become Buxton Woods—now the largest maritime forest remaining on the Outer Banks—had begun.

By the time the first Europeans arrived, Buxton Woods was a ten-thousand-acre forest that covered half of the highlands near Cape Hatteras. Live oaks and loblolly pines had joined the cedars, and a dense understory of vines, dogwoods, holly, yaupon, and other salt-tolerant plants thrived in the thin layer of humus that now covered the sandy, nutrient-poor soil. To those early Europeans, the dense forests appeared amazingly fertile.

In his history of the Outer Banks, David Stick quotes Captain Arthur Barlowe, an emissary of Sir Walter Raleigh, who visited the area in 1584, going ashore not far north of Hatteras: "This Island had many goodly woods full of Deere, Conies, Hares, and Fowle, even in the middest of Summer, in incredible aboundance . . . [and] the highest, and reddest Cedars of the world."

Based on this glowing report and others like it, the English attempted to establish a permanent settlement on Roanoke Island, just inland of Hatteras. In 1587, after several false starts, an expedition led by John White left 112 men, women, and children on the northern tip of Roanoke Island with instructions to establish the "Cittie of Raleigh." When White, the grandfather of Virginia Dare—the first English child born in America—returned in 1590, the colonists had vanished, leaving only the word *Croatoan* carved in a post near their fort. White took the message to mean that the colonists had fled across the sound to Croatoan—now called Hatteras Island—but of course they were never found.

If the ill-fated settlers did make it to Hatteras Island, they would have cut down trees in the maritime forest to provide wood for their fires, logs for their houses. And the destruction of Buxton Woods, which may have started with the lost colonists, continues to this day. The forest has been whittled down to 3,000 acres, 920 of which are part of Cape Hatteras National Seashore. The state of North Carolina owns nearly 500 acres, but half of the woods is private property, and the salty sea air that blows through "the highest, and reddest Cedars of the world" is rife with talk of golf courses and condos and water slides.

The trail through these woods passes through three distinct ecosystems. The walk starts on Buxton Woods Trail, which meanders through the verdant maritime forest that lies south of Jennette Sedge. About halfway to Frisco Campground, the trail enters a sandy, almost treeless area sprinkled with dune grass and shrubs, where (I suspect) logging and livestock grazing have eradicated nearly all traces of the forest that once stood there. During this part of the walk, relict dunes—the sandy skeleton of Hatteras disguised in years past by the skin of forest overlaying it—show clearly. Finally, the walk concludes on Hatteras's most famous ecosystem—the beach.

I take this walk on a cool day in early spring when the Carolina jasmine, having twined its way up the trunks of the forest trees, ornaments their crowns with bright yellow flowers. Buxton Woods is an evergreen maritime forest, dark with live oaks and pines, but hornbeams and a few other deciduous trees also grow here. The delicate light green of their new leaves brightens the forest and, along with the jasmine, makes it easy to remember that it's really spring.

Not far from the trailhead, I spot a yaupon, a shrubby member of the holly family (genus *Ilex*) that is found in North Carolina only near the coast. The plant is common in the maritime forest and produces beautiful red berries in the winter, which I'm told Outer Banks residents—"Bankers"— use for Christmas decorations. It is a small, undistinguished tree, rarely twenty feet tall, but I like it because of its scientific name, surely one of the more graphic ever assigned: *I. vomitoria*.

The Indians made a tea from the leaves and twigs of *I. vomitoria* which, living up to its name, induced vomiting and acted as a laxative. Considering its effects, yaupon tea was a surprisingly popular brew. In his *New Voyage to Carolina*, published in 1709, John Lawson, that hardy traveler and surveyor-general of North Carolina, writes that the tea was "us'd and approv'd by all the Savages on the coast of *Carolina*, and from them sent to the Westward *Indians*, and sold at a considerable price." He then goes on to admit that he has tried yaupon tea himself and liked it pretty well.

According to Lawson, the Indians took it "every other Morning, or oftner," drinking it "in vast Quantities . . . and vomiting it up again, as clear as they drink it." Yaupon tea also became popular with the settlers along the coast, perhaps because they had few alternatives. According to David Stick, one man in Frisco was operating a "yappon factory" as late as 1903.

The tea's popularity with Bankers both red and white may have stemmed from its medicinal properties, but the caffeine in its leaves probably had something to do with it, too. And of course, the ingredients—water and yaupon—were free. But its appeal was not its taste. More or less following Lawson's directions, I once brewed a batch of the stuff. It was greenish brown and very bitter.

Farther up the trail, I find the yaupon's cousin, American holly, mixed in with the bays and dogwoods and wax myrtles that are common in this maritime forest. A cattail-rimmed freshwater sedge lies to the right of the trail.

Because the dunes in this part of Buxton Woods once lined the beach, they occur as ridges running from east to west. Sedges form when rainwater collects in the valleys between the ridges. Because the freshwater table is just a few feet below the surface—a few inches in some places—the sedges stay wet even in dry weather, and complex freshwater ecosystems develop in them. The result is a community of creatures usually found far inland—frogs, toads, cottonmouths, and others—living almost within earshot of the surf.

Another plant along the trail is the dwarf palmetto (*Sabal minor*). Except for Nags Head Woods, a maritime forest fifty or so miles to the north, Buxton Woods is the northernmost extent of the palm family on the East Coast. Like the sedge, the dwarf palmetto's presence can be traced to the sea. Because

Hatteras juts so far eastward, currents from the north-flowing Gulf Stream brush the island's shores. The warm currents temper the climate, enabling this hardy palm to survive winters at a latitude that would otherwise kill it.

After two miles, the trail leaves the forest. The transition is abrupt, and without the shade of the trees, the sun feels hot and the trail sand seems deeper. Ries Collier, a biologist with Cape Hatteras National Seashore, says he's not sure what happened

to this land, says he's not sure how this large, desertlike patch of dunes came to exist in the maritime forest. But I think I might know. This section of Hatteras looks very much like parts of Shackleford Banks, the barrier island lying just west of Core Banks.

Shackleford Banks is part of Cape Lookout National Seashore now, but when my family used to go there, the island was privately owned. In pre-European times, a maritime forest covered much of it. Then a few settlers took up residence. The island was never heavily populated, though, and by 1902, everyone was gone, driven to the mainland by the devastating hurricane of 1899. Unfortunately, they left their livestock behind. Goats and sheep and horses and at least one magnificent black bull roamed the island. Their grazing destroyed the grasses whose roots anchored the dunes. Driven by the prevailing winds, the dunes migrated inland. Like tiny, out-of-control bumper cars, the grains of sand stopped and re-formed as dunes only when they hit something solid—like the trees and shrubs of the maritime forest.

By the early 1970s, most of Shackleford's woods were gone, either buried under dunes or recently emerged from them as the lifeless stumps of a dead forest. There is no dead forest along Buxton Woods Trail, but time or logging could account for its absence. In any case, this nearly bare section of Hatteras looks much like the destroyed interior of Shackleford Banks in the seventies, and I suspect its history is similar, too.

Buxton Woods Trail ends at Frisco Campground. A weathered gray boardwalk leads through the dunes to the beach. The sun is hot, but a cooling breeze blows off the ocean. Pelicans and sandpipers and ring-billed gulls stand idly on the beach, and dolphins surface just beyond the breakers. The spring shore teems with life, and after the hot sand and soft dunes of the interior, I love the prospect of a long walk on the hard sand by the edge of the sea.

But the sea is also a place of death. A mile later, I spot a large bird near the high-tide line. It is dead but shows no signs of injury. The bird is white with black wing tips and a large blue bill. It is a gannet, the first I've ever seen. Gannets spend most of their time over the water and rarely come ashore in North Carolina. Later, I learn that twenty gannets were found dead that year on the beaches of the Outer Banks, that severe storms, a lack of food, and the general stresses of winter probably killed the birds at sea, and they washed ashore along with the seashells and beach wrack.

Not far beyond the gannet, I spot a bird whose liveliness rejuvenates me. It, too, is black and white, but its long red bill unmistakably identifies it as an oystercatcher.

Oystercatchers are common along the seashores of North Carolina. But these big, showy wading birds are ordinarily quite wary and difficult to approach, so as soon as I see it, I freeze. The one I am watching is soon joined by another. They are less than fifty feet from me, and I have the rare opportunity to observe a pair of oystercatchers going about their daily business.

Oystercatchers usually feed on, well, oysters, at least in the South. Their favorite prey is a small bivalve known as the coon oyster (because raccoons like to eat them, too). The birds pry open oysters and other shellfish with their flattened, chisel-like bills and sever the adductor muscles that clamp the bivalves' two shells together. But the birds I'm watching aren't feeding on oysters; they are running about the beach like oversized sandpipers, sinking their bills deeply in the wet sand and probing for worms and small mollusks. Their quick, sure movements entrance me, but after a few minutes I inadvertently move, and the oystercatchers fly off, wheeling over the breakers, chiding me with raucous cries.

What does it take to be a naturalist? Being able to stand very still helps, but sometimes that's not enough. In *Birds of America*, Herbert Job illustrates this point when he explains how he photographed an oystercatcher on its nest:

> *The open sand-flat afforded no possible concealment. At night I placed a bunch of seaweed near the two eggs. In the morning I set a camera under this, and, attaching a spool of strong thread to the shutter, had my friends bury me in the sand . . . all but my head and arm. When the rest of the party left the island, the birds walked right past me, gazing without fear at the apparently disconnected head cast up by the waves. Soon the female was shielding her eggs from the blazing Carolina sun. Then I excitedly pulled the thread and the picture was mine!*

That's what it takes to be a naturalist!

The last mile or two go quickly. Like so many others over the last one hundred or so years, I use the Cape Hatteras Lighthouse as a reference to gauge my position. I glance at the tiny map I'm carrying, and when the angle between shore and lighthouse look right, I tack northeast off the beach onto a tangle of sand roads used by surf fishermen. Minutes later, I'm at Buxton Campground, closed and deserted at this time of year.

In guiding me here, the old lighthouse has once again served its purpose. The scientists who predicted its end were undoubtedly right: the Cape Hatteras Lighthouse is a goner. The eastern shore of Hatteras is eroding. When the lighthouse was built, it was five hundred yards from the ocean; today, it is less than seventy. The latest prediction is that unless the lighthouse is moved, it will be gone by the year 2000, a victim of change—the one constant in the islands.

Which leads to the question being pondered by the National Park Service: should the lighthouse be moved? I believe it should. To let nature take its course by allowing this beautiful and famous lighthouse to fall into the Atlantic makes no more sense than leaving the art of Venice hanging on the walls of the Accademia as the waters of the Grand Canal rise.

Before You Go

For More Information _____
Cape Hatteras National Seashore
Route 1, Box 675
Manteo, N.C. 27954
(919) 473-2111

Accommodations _____
Outer Banks Chamber of Commerce
P.O. Box 1757
Kill Devil Hills, N.C. 27984
(919) 441-8144

Campgrounds _____
Five campgrounds are scattered along the length of Cape Hatteras National Seashore. Buxton and Frisco campgrounds are close to Buxton Woods and make ideal starting points for this walk. The

campgrounds are only open during the summer season, and they can be crowded. Reservations are not accepted at either campground.

Maps _____

There are no maps which show the details of Buxton Woods Trail. The two United States Geological Survey maps that cover the area are Cape Hatteras and Buxton.

Additional Reading

The Beaches Are Moving: The Drowning of America's Shoreline by Wallace Kaufman and Orrin H. Pilkey, Jr., Duke University Press, Durham, N.C., 1983.

Birds of America by T. Gilbert Pearson, Garden City Books, Garden City, N.Y., 1936.

Life Histories of North American Shorebirds, part 2, by Arthur Cleveland Bent, Dover Publications, New York, 1962. This book was originally published in 1929 as Smithsonian Institution United States National Museum *Bulletin 146.*

A New Voyage to Carolina by John Lawson, edited with an introduction and notes by Hugh Talmage Lefler, University of North Carolina Press, Chapel Hill, 1967.

The Outer Banks of North Carolina by David Stick, University of North Carolina Press, Chapel Hill, 1958.

Ribbon of Sand by John Alexander and James Lazell, Algonquin Books of Chapel Hill, Chapel Hill, N.C., 1992.

Length: 6.6 miles

**Degree
of Difficulty: Easy to Moderate**

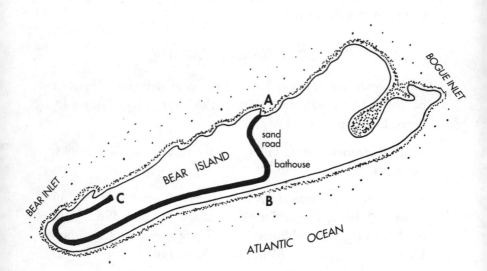

Bear Island Walk

A.   Ferry dock
B.   Beach
C.   Trail ends

Route and Distances

A. to B.	Sand road to beach	0.6 mi.
B. to C.	Walk along beach and marsh	2.7 mi.
C. to A.	Return	3.3 mi.
	TOTAL	6.6 mi.

Beach and Marsh

Bear Island
Hammocks Beach State Park

The ferry from the mainland to Bear Island leaves from the Hammocks Beach State Park office at the end of State Road 1511, off N.C. 24 near Swansboro. The walk starts at the ferry dock on Bear Island. From the dock, a sand road leads to the ocean. Proceed west on the beach to Bear Inlet. An unmarked trail runs northeast around the point and ends in the marsh after 0.5 mile. Return the way you came.

Seven o'clock in the morning. We're headed east on I-40, past the busyness of the Research Triangle, then Raleigh. This is a new road, maybe the best stretch of interstate in the country. Beyond Benson, the traffic is lighter, so I press heavier on the accelerator; we pass Newton Grove and Mount Olive. We exit onto N.C. 24 and slow down for Kenansville and Beaulaville, sleepy and still in the early morning. Then there's Jacksonville with its drive-in pawn shops and topless bars. Soon, they, too,

disappear, replaced by fields of corn and soybeans, patches of tobacco and pine woods. Pickup trucks with their windows down replace Camaros with darkened glass and air conditioning. We're deep in the country now, but where we're going is even more remote. We make Swansboro a little before nine. Perfect: the first ferry to Bear Island leaves at nine-thirty.

Hammocks Beach State Park consists of 35 acres of mainland and 892-acre Bear Island. We're here to explore the beaches and marshes of that island, one of the few never-developed links in the chain of barrier islands that runs from New Jersey to Florida. I have a guide for this walk; my son, Michael, worked here last summer, researching and writing a history of the park. As far as he's concerned, this is *his* island.

Two laughing young men in tan uniforms pilot the ferry through a channel in the salt marsh. Egrets fleck the green spartina, and an osprey watches from a dead pine. Gulls follow the ferry, hoping for handouts, and terns search the water for telltale disturbances. The morning is cool, the water quiet.

From the ferry dock on the sound side of Bear Island, we begin the walk to the beach. It's a little over a half-mile across the island. The road is sandy, and the vegetation is scrub mixed with low-lying trees. A maritime forest rises in the distance. Where the road slices through the dunes to meet the beach, there is a combination bathhouse and concession stand. Some sunbathers have raced across the island in front of us. They crowd into a hundred yards of seashore. Beyond them in either direction lies emptiness—no towels, no suntan oil, no people, just foaming breakers pounding a broad beach.

Even at mid-tide, the beach is as wide as I-40 and almost as bare. Since there are no full-time residents on the island and, for a state park, few visitors, there is almost no litter. And because of some peculiarity of tide and current, even beach wrack and seashells are scarce. In fact, some historians claim that the original spelling was *Bare* Island.

We head southwest, walking easily on the firm, grainy shore. A willet pecks in the sand at the water's edge, and a line of grassy foredunes ten or fifteen feet high runs endlessly down the beach. The row of dunes looks steady and stable, and like the wall of a fort, it presents a bland, strong face to its enemy, the churning sea.

Since the last Ice Age, sea levels have been generally rising as melt pours into the oceans. Geologists believe that North Carolina's barrier islands appeared a few thousand years ago when the sea's rise slowed and became intermittent, punctuated by periods of stable and even decreasing sea levels. Sand bars which had been accumulating for thousands of years inched above the sea's surface.

Because they are composed almost entirely of sand, barrier islands tend to be unstable, increasing or decreasing in size, and even moving about, depending on the strength and direction of the tides and currents and winds. Inlets also come and go, cutting channels through the islands, then closing them, as storms and hurricanes batter the coast. But Bear Island has been remarkably enduring. There is no record that it has ever been much different from the way it is today, and it owes its stability to those grassy foredunes, unmolested over the years, that protect the island from the sea.

Although the dunes appear solid, a closer look shows that both they and the beach are actually riddled with holes, giving the island the look of a sandy Swiss cheese. A few minutes later, we see one of the hole-diggers; a ghost crab with heavy, pale claws held high scuttles by, looking for its burrow. Michael tells me that when he worked here, the staff used to come down to the water at night with flashlights to watch the thousands of crabs that patrol the beach in the darkness. Bear Island, it turns out, is a perfect ghost-crab habitat.

In one of those odd but sometimes useful experiments forever denounced as boondoggles by watchdog groups of indignant citizens, scientists measured the density of ghost crabs on a number of beaches. Completely wild beaches—those where humans were not allowed at all—averaged ten ghost crabs per eighteen square meters. The density almost doubled on beaches where people were allowed, but it dropped to less than one per square meter if vehicles were permitted.

Ghost crabs (*Ocypode quadrata*) are categorized as "opportunistic omnivores"—they'll eat anything. The scientists speculated that sunbathers and pedestrians drop bits of food which the ghost crabs devour, allowing their numbers to increase. But cars crush the crabs in their burrows. And since people may visit Bear Island but cars cannot, the result is ghost-crab paradise.

The earliest crabs were sea dwellers that lived over one hundred million years ago. Ghost crabs came along later, but their lives are still linked to the sea. Though the adults of the species dig their burrows in the dry sand of the upper beach, ghost crabs are not air-breathers; they have gills.

In *The Edge of the Sea*, Rachel Carson describes the development of a ghost crab:

The larva . . . is oceanic, becoming a creature of the plankton once it has hatched. . . . As the infant crab drifts in the currents it sheds its cuticle several times to accommodate the increasing size of its body ... [until] the last larval stage is reached. This is the form in which all the destiny of the race is symbolized, for it—a tiny creature alone in the sea—must obey whatever instinct drives it shoreward, and must make a successful landing on the beach.

Once ashore, the crab digs its burrows farther and farther from the sea. Yet it cannot escape its origins. Females must return to the water to lay their eggs, and several times a day, every ghost crab must immerse its gills in life-giving salt water. Since ghost crabs leave their holes reluctantly during the daylight hours, the one we see is likely returning from such a mission.

As we continue down the beach, Michael points out small, nondescript plants growing between the high-tide line and the foredunes. Barrier islands are rough on plants, but the no man's land between surf and dune—with its salt spray and shifting sands and periodic flooding—is especially rugged. The vegetation here is sparse and hunkered down, the plant species so uncommon that even user-friendly texts refer to them only by their scientific names: *Amaranthus pumilus, Sesuvium maritimum,* and so forth.

These fragile plants—long gone from many of our beaches—survive on Bear Island because it has never been developed. Its nearly untouched state is due to the absence of a bridge and its distance from the population centers on the coast. It also lacks a harbor and any other natural resources worth developing. For those reasons, Bear Island has played only a minor role in the swirl of human events.

In the early 1800s, a blubber-rendering station was built on the island to take advantage of the whales that regularly beached themselves here. And during the Civil War, the Confederate army dispatched a few guards to protect Bear Island from attack by Union troops. But there was no attack, and the soldiers were withdrawn within a few months. Sometime later, Union forces did land on the island to rescue forty-three escaped slaves who were hiding here. That was not the last time the island would provide temporary refuge for Southern blacks.

Today, Bear Island is also a haven for creatures other than man, a place to nest and rest and escape persecution. As Michael and I walk down the beach, we see the blue plastic stakes that mark the nests of the most celebrated of the island's visitors: the loggerhead turtles.

Loggerheads are sea turtles, creatures with an evolutionary history that is the mirror image of the ghost crabs'. They are land animals that adopted the sea.

Female loggerheads—huge, barnacle-encrusted animals weighing up to three hundred pounds—lumber ashore at night, usually at high tide during a full moon, to lay about one hundred golf-ball-sized eggs in cylindrical nests they dig in the sand. When the eggs hatch, the baby turtles must climb through the foot or so of sand which the female has scraped over the eggs and compacted with her belly. Then they make a mad dash for the sea. For the males, the beach they cross between nest and ocean will be their only contact with dry land for the rest of their lives. But that brief period ashore—from the moment the mother deposits her eggs until the hatchlings are in the surf—is the most vulnerable time in the sea turtles' life.

Unlike the green turtle, which is poached for its flesh and its calipee (the cartilage from its bottom shell that is used in soup), adult loggerheads have few enemies. Some drown when they are accidentally caught in the nets of shrimpers and fishermen, but laws mandating the use of Turtle Excluding Devices (TEDs) are reducing those casualties. Development along the beaches where they nest is probably the major cause of the decline of loggerheads. Lights from nearby highways and houses confuse nesting turtles and distract emerging hatchlings from their beeline to the surf. But on an undeveloped island like this one, the biggest danger to the turtles comes not from men but from beasts.

Raccoons love loggerhead eggs. They detect the nests by smell and, according to Archie Carr, "harvest them with deadly efficiency." In his book, *So Excellent a Fishe*, Carr describes a nesting site near Cape Sable in Everglades National Park where raccoons destroyed 140 of 199 loggerhead nests.

To combat the coons on Bear Island, Michael tells me, the Turtle Man (as he or she is called) hits the beach at six o'clock every morning, searching for the furrows that nesting loggerheads leave in the sand when they crawl ashore. When he finds a track, he locates the nest and covers it with a square of chicken wire to foil the raccoons, using long staples to fasten the wire to the ground. He then drives a plastic stake into the sand to warn humans away. Michael says the technique works; during his summer here, over thirty loggerhead nests were counted, and none was lost to raccoons—or to humans.

Ghost crabs are another story. Loggerhead hatchlings make their run for the sea at night, and that's when the ghost-crab patrol is out. Nobody knows exactly what toll this gauntlet takes on the silver-dollar-sized turtles, but given the number of crab burrows that perforate the island, it is probably significant.

Farther down the beach, we see signs and birds on the sandy spit that marks the end of the island. Beyond it, Bear Inlet runs shallow and swift, building up sand bars here, tearing them down there. A faint trail bends around the point, following the shoreline of the sound. This side of the island is as different from the beach as an oasis is from a desert. Much of the lushness is due to the grass, an arc of bright green that cups the backside of the island. This is cordgrass, *Spartina alterniflora*, and it does for Bear Island what mangrove trees do for Florida, trapping organic deposits and building the rich, muddy floor needed for a healthy marsh.

On this part of the island, the land rises steeply. Just a few feet from the water, a maritime forest grows on the high ground. As we continue around the back of the island, the path becomes fainter, threading its way between marsh and forest, and it soon peters out entirely. At the end of the trail, an unusually tall loblolly pine rises out of an impenetrable tangle of morning glories and shrubs. The smell of bay trees mingles with the sharp scent of salt marsh. Michael takes a deep breath, drops his knapsack, and sinks to the sand. "This is as far as it goes," he says. "How about lunch?"

I produce sandwiches, and we dig in, sitting in the sand, looking out over the marsh. Down here, at grass level, we can see limpets clinging to the blades of spartina, waiting for the food the next high tide will bring. The air is lazy, quieter and warmer than it was on the beach, and we rest for a while.

On the way back, we stop at the point to read the signs we saw earlier. Michael posted these signs last year, but even if he didn't know what they said, the dive-bombing terns would give us an unmistakable clue.

COLONIAL SEABIRD NESTING AREA
KEEP OUT

The attacking birds are least terns, sometimes called sea swallows because of their forked tails and graceful, agile flight. They are pale birds, light gray and white, slightly smaller than robins. They lay their eggs in shallow depressions on the sandy beach between the dunes and the storm-tide line. If you get close to their nests, they will hover over your head and dive at you with sharp cries of warning. According to Lynn Mosely, a graduate student who studied least terns for four summers, the birds frequently defecate at the end of such dives. She commented on this habit in her thesis but did not find it unusual. It's the sort of thing graduate students get used to.

But if Mosely got used to the birds, they never got used to her. She reported that they attacked her with as much enthusiasm after four years as they did when she started her study. Least

terns don't like people near their nesting sites, and their preju-
dice is well founded. We almost wiped them out.

The slaughter started before the turn of the century, and the
reason for it was the millinery trade. The least terns' delicate
white feathers added a nice touch to the fine hats of fashionable
women.

As with most birds, least terns' plumage is at its finest during
the summer breeding season, so the birds were hunted then.
That is also when the terns, their eggs, and their young are the
most vulnerable.

Least terns breed in colonies along the Atlantic coast from
Cape Cod to the Florida Keys and on the Gulf coast from
Florida to Texas. Their habit of trying to bluff predators with
their fluttering dives played into the hands of market hunters,
who shot millions of them and left the terns' unhatched eggs to
rot on the beach and their unfledged young to starve. The dead
birds were packed in cracked ice and sent to New York. The
hunters got a dime a bird, and for that price they sent the least
tern well down the road to extinction.

The sequence of events that saved them began around the
turn of the century. The most important of these was the
incorporation of the Audubon Society in 1905. By the end of
that year, the so-called Audubon Law—a wild-bird protection
act—had been passed in thirty-three states. That legislation,
coupled with the nascent National Wildlife Refuge system set
up two years earlier by President Theodore Roosevelt, protected non-game birds and no doubt saved the least tern—and the
egret, heron, and flamingo—from extirpation in this country.

As we walk down the beach back to the ferry, the sun pops
out of the overcast. The weather has been perfect, one of those

rare cool days in June. The sunlight turns the white dunes into shimmering mirages. There's a steady breeze and no bugs. Michael says the weather must have been this good in 1914 when Dr. William Sharpe first visited the island, because he liked the place so much he bought it. Sharpe's purchase led to a series of events that ended up protecting this island—and its least-tern nesting sites—forever. And soon after the purchase, our country enacted legislation even more significant than the Audubon Law to right a wrong that had existed longer than market hunting.

Sharpe was a New York neurosurgeon who enjoyed hunting and fishing. To pursue those pastimes, he bought Bear Island and 4,600 acres on the mainland. He hired John Hurst, a local black man, to look after his properties. After World War II, Sharpe—a generous and concerned man—offered to give the island to Hurst and his wife, Gertrude, in gratitude for their years of service.

Mrs. Hurst, a schoolteacher, suggested that it be given instead to the North Carolina Teachers Association, a nonprofit group of black educators. Sharpe agreed, and in 1950 the property was transferred to the N.C.T.A. on the condition that it be used to provide recreational and educational opportunities for blacks. To meet those terms, the N.C.T.A. created the Hammocks Beach Corporation and charged it with the task of satisfying the deed.

Segregation was legal in those days, and blacks were not allowed to visit most North Carolina parks, so Sharpe's gift was a welcome one. All the N.C.T.A. had to do was figure out how to use it.

The problem was transportation. Although the Hammocks

Beach Corporation quickly raised a hundred thousand dollars, the cost of a bridge was over a million. They asked the state to help, but the state declined. Then they offered to *give* the island to the state for use as a park for blacks if the state would build a bridge. Again, the state declined. Since the corporation could not satisfy the conditions of its deed, it appeared that Bear Island would have to be returned to the Sharpe family, that its isolation would once again keep the world at bay.

But the N.C.T.A. did not give up. The Hammocks Beach Corporation made one more try. In 1958, the corporation withdrew its demand for a bridge and offered the state the property for use as a park if it would dredge a channel and establish ferry service to the island. Finally, the state agreed, and in 1961 Hammocks Beach State Park, North Carolina's third black state park, opened. Three years later, the Civil Rights Act ended racial segregation on public property and opened all parks to blacks and whites alike.

By the time Michael finishes the story, we have reached the road that leads back to the dock. We join the trickle of day-trippers headed toward the waiting ferry.

During the ride back to the mainland, several least terns flash in front of the boat, searching the greenish brown water for food. A class of brown and black and white second-graders race around the boat, yelling at one another, laughing, having second-grade fun. Michael stands at the bow, watching the terns through his binoculars. One of the boys, wearing shorts and a red Michael Jordan tank top, sidles over and asks to look. Michael hands him the glasses.

"That a sea gull?" the kid asks.

"No," Michael says. "It's a least tern."

"Bet he be good to eat. Can you shoot 'em?"

Michael tries to look stern. "No, it's against the law to kill them."

"Like the turtles?"

"Yeah, like the turtles."

"That's okay," says the kid, handing the binoculars back. "Our teacher say the law helps the turtles, but there still not be any 'cept this island so far in the sticks."

"Maybe," says Michael. "Isolation's good for turtles and terns. But laws help, too."

"Right," says the kid, moving away to join his friends. "You right about that."

Before You Go

For More Information ————————————————
Hammocks Beach State Park
14000 Hammocks Beach Road
Swansboro, N.C. 28584
(919) 326-4881

Accommodations ————————————————
Jacksonville/Onslow County Chamber of Commerce
P.O. Box 765
1 Marine Boulevard North
Jacksonville, N.C. 28541
(919) 347-3141

Campgrounds ————————————————
There are fourteen individual campsites and three group sites on Bear Island. Camping is not permitted around the full moons of June, July, and August to avoid disturbing nesting loggerheads. The length

and timing of these closings vary from year to year. Get a schedule before you go. Reservations for campsites may be made through the park office.

Maps

The park brochure includes a map that is adequate for this walk.

Special Precautions

Soft drinks and light snacks are sold at the concession stand on Bear Island. If you want anything else, you'll have to bring it with you.

The ferry runs every hour or half-hour (depending on the crowds) during the summer only; a schedule is available from the park.

Points of Interest

To see what can happen to a barrier island with bridges to the mainland, you might want to visit Bogue Banks, the island just east of Bear Island. You won't see any turtle nests, but you will find suntan lotion, beer, and condominiums.

Additional Reading

Barrier Island Handbook by Stephen P. Leatherman, National Park Service Cooperative Research Unit, Environmental Institute, University of Massachusetts, Amherst, 1979.

"Behavior and Communication in the Least Tern" by Lynn J. Mosely, master's thesis, University of North Carolina at Chapel Hill, 1976.

Biology of the Land Crabs edited by Warren W. Burggren and Brian R. McMahon, Cambridge University Press, Cambridge, England, 1988.

The Edge of the Sea by Rachel Carson, Houghton Mifflin Company, Boston, 1955.

"History of Bear Island" by Michael Manning, unpublished, available on request from the park office.

Life Histories of North American Gulls and Terns by Arthur Cleveland Bent, Dover Publications, New York, 1963. The original edition of this book was published in 1921 as Smithsonian Institution *Bulletin 113.*

So Excellent a Fishe: A Natural History of Sea Turtles by Archie Carr, Natural History Press, Garden City, N.Y., 1967.

Wildlife in America by Peter Matthiessen, Viking Penguin, New York, 1987.

Length: 6 miles

**Degree
of Difficulty: Easy**

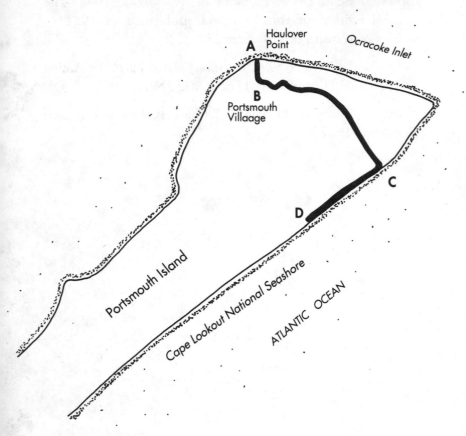

Portsmouth Island Walk

A.	Boat dock at Haulover Point
B.	Portsmouth Village
C.	Beach
D.	Turn-around point

Route and Distances

A. to B.	Road to Portsmouth Village	0.4 mi.
B. to C.	Road through salt flats to beach	1.6 mi.
C. to D	Walk along beach	1.0 mi.
D. to A.	Return	3.0 mi.
	TOTAL	6.0 mi.

The Salt Flats

Portsmouth Island
Cape Lookout National Seashore

Access to Cape Lookout National Seashore is by boat only. To reach Portsmouth Island, contact Junius Austin in Ocracoke at (919) 928-4281. In 1992, a round trip between Ocracoke and Portsmouth islands cost $35 for one person and $5 more for each additional person up to a total of six. From the National Park Service ferry dock at Haulover Point, a sand road leads to Portsmouth village. The road continues southeast through the village to the edge of the salt flats, where a signed path leads to the sea. Proceed southwest down the beach for 1 mile (about 20 minutes at normal beach-walking speed) before returning the way you came. For a longer walk, you can continue on the beach for up to 4 more miles to Whalebone Inlet.

The village of Portsmouth, once the largest seaport on the Outer Banks, is a ghost town. And as with other ghost towns, nostalgic stories surround it. Stories about the day the post office closed for good. Sto-  ries about the last occupant and the last funeral. Stories of its early years, its good years, and finally of its long, sad decline. Official documents and scholarly papers detail the village's cultural history and attempt to explain the dramatic changes that took it from boom town to oblivion. But the natural history of the island, the narrative told by the land and the life that lives on it, is less well known, and even the casual naturalist can see that the land tells a different story, one of constancy rather than change. Surprisingly, Portsmouth Island's turbulent human history seems to have touched the land only lightly.

Today, Portsmouth Island is part of Cape Lookout National Seashore, fifty-five miles of barrier islands that also include Core Banks and Shackleford Banks. The island is little more than a sand bar, a wide, low-lying beach, a gappy row of foredunes, a vast expanse of tidal flats, 250 acres of high ground, and finally, near the sound, marshland. It's a fine place for fiddler crabs, cordgrass, and sea oats, for birds and raccoons and mosquitoes, but it's hardly an ideal spot for a town.

A village was established on the island in the mid-eighteenth century because the Ocracoke-Portsmouth inlet was the only inlet on North Carolina's northern coast deep enough for oceangoing ships. All freight into and out of the ports along the Roanoke, Pamlico, and Neuse rivers had to pass through that inlet. Unfortunately, the channel leading north to Ocracoke Harbor and Pamlico Sound was too serpentine and too shallow to accommodate heavily loaded oceangoing ships. To get goods to and from the growing towns along the northern rivers, shippers were forced to anchor offshore and transfer their cargo to smaller boats—a practice known as lightering. The off-loaded freight was then ferried ashore and stored in warehouses for transshipment to its final destination.

All that was needed for lightering were some boats, a warehouse or two, a few good seafaring men, and some land on which to base them. That land, the colonial assembly decreed in 1753, would be Portsmouth Island.

The assembly reasoned that since Portsmouth Island lies south of Ocracoke Inlet, large vessels could anchor near the island without having to cross the shallows to the northeast, known as Ocracoke Swash. The island also had a few acres of high ground, upon which warehouses and a town could be built. It is unlikely that any members of the assembly—which met in New Bern—had ever set foot on Portsmouth Island, but with the bland assurance of government officials everywhere, they acted. And so the village of Portsmouth was born.

To get to the island these days, you contact Junius Austin in Ocracoke. After a phone call, I agree to meet him at Crystal Lake. Fifteen minutes later, an old but freshly painted twenty-five-foot wooden inboard eases up to the dock. Junius is a dignified, compact man of about sixty with gray hair and the kind of tan that comes from a life spent on the water. His movements about the boat are precise and spare, with no wasted motion. Everything about him suggests competence. Junius used to live on Portsmouth Island, and he knows the secret, twisting channels of Ocracoke Swash as well as any man. Since I have tried—unsuccessfully—to negotiate the swash in my own boat, I'm happy to leave the driving to him.

It's a bright, calm day. Junius maneuvers through the narrow channels without seeming to touch the wheel. Twenty minutes later, he deposits me at the National Park Service dock at Haulover Point, the northernmost tip of Portsmouth Island. The landscape is scruffy brush and marsh; the early-spring air smells of salt water and swamp gas. A yaupon-lined sand road leads south to the village. An army of fiddler crabs, each soldier brandishing one large claw, defends the path.

For a few minutes, I watch the crabs scuttle about on the sand. They move sideways, holding their one outsized pincer high in front of them like tiny fighters ready for combat. The fighter simile is an old one. Louis Bosc, who also observed these crabs on the Carolina shore, must have had that image in mind in 1802 when he named them *Uca pugilator*.

But the name fits only superficially. Fiddlers rarely fight, either among themselves or with other creatures. In fact, the large claw is used primarily as a sexual attractor. The males wave it above their heads to entice females into their burrows.

When I start toward the village, the fiddlers in the road vanish into pellet-rimmed holes. They disappear quietly, and like the lightermen who once plied their trade from Haulover Point, few signs of their lives remain. But the crabs were here first, and in a reversal of the usual trend, they have endured and the people have vanished. It's hard to believe that busy warehouses once stood along this road where fiddler crabs now live, that Portsmouth village, with a population today of zero, was a bustling community of nearly seven hundred before the Civil War.

I stroll through the village past trim lawns shaded by stately red cedars. The National Park Service leases a few houses in Portsmouth to its employees and to solitude seekers in exchange for keeping up the grounds. The twenty or so houses still standing are simple, well-maintained one- or two-story clapboard structures. Each one has a sign out front with its name on it. There's the Dixon-Salter House (now a National Park Service visitor center and closed this time of year). There's the Post Office-General Store and the School House and the Methodist Church. Next to Doctors Creek sits Henry Pigott's house. Pigott's death in 1971 reduced the population of Portsmouth to two, and Elma Dixon and Marian Babb, concerned about living on the island without a man around, soon left for the mainland.

The lifesaving station is the last building you pass on the way to the beach. Once, twenty-five such stations were located up and down the Outer Banks of North Carolina—ample testimony to the reality behind the cliché "Graveyard of the Atlantic." Behind the large doors of the gray-shingled building, surfmen and their boats once stood ready to charge into the deadly storms that periodically wrack these islands and the offshore shipping lanes. The Portsmouth station, which in 1903 rescued 421 passengers from the wrecked *Vera Cruz II*, was closed in 1937.

Beyond the station, the road continues east toward the beach. The trees disappear. Shrubs become smaller and sparser, and a quarter of a mile later, they, too, vanish. In front of me lie the great tidal flats of Portsmouth Island, bare sand that extends for miles. Directly ahead, I can barely make out an irregular line of dunes along the beach. Between me and the dunes, the landscape is as level and as empty as the salt flats of Utah.

Though the flats look barren, life flourishes in environments far harsher than this. Anaerobic bacteria live in sulfur vents at the bottom of the sea; lichens cling to rocks beneath snow high above the tree line; and some species of brine shrimp thrive in the incredible salinity of Great Salt Lake. So it's no surprise to find bird and raccoon tracks in the sand, to stand quietly and watch ghost crabs and fiddlers edge cautiously out of their holes, to glimpse sea oats on the tops of the dunes. Although the biodiversity of a tidal flat will never rival that of a lush hardwood cove, there is life here. But you must look carefully and be patient to find it.

It's about a mile across the flats to the beach. Northerly winds, storms, and very high tides flood these flats with ankle-deep water, but the weather has been calm recently, and the sand is dry and firm beneath my feet. Halfway across, the cries of gulls and terns replace the raspy voices of the grackles and crows that followed me through the village. As I near the beach, I see ring-bills loafing on the shore while a half-dozen least terns work the water just behind the breakers. A cormorant whizzes by, flying low over the water.

At the ocean, I turn and walk southwest down the shore. From here, you used to be able to walk the twenty miles to Drum Inlet without getting your feet wet. But no more. Because they lie so low in the sea, Portsmouth Island and Core Banks are especially subject to overwashes. New inlets form today and fill tomorrow, and my map tells me that Whalebone and Swash inlets are now the first two interruptions farther down the beach. Although inlet creation and closure are particularly common on Portsmouth Island and Core Banks, major storms and hurricanes can alter the topography anywhere along the Outer Banks.

The storm that started Portsmouth on the path to commercial oblivion struck in 1846. Historian David Stick quotes Redding Quidley, who was there when the storm hit. "Hatteras Inlet," Quidley said, "was cut out by a heavy gale, a violent storm" that struck the night of September 7. The next day, four fathoms of water covered the land where Quidley had chopped wood the day before. He went on to tell about other families that lived near the new inlet and to describe their surprise when "they saw the sea and sound connected together, and the live oaks washing up by the roots and tumbling into the ocean." Five months later, Quidley piloted the first boat through Hatteras Inlet. A new, navigable route into Pamlico Sound now existed nearly twenty miles northeast of Portsmouth Island.

After I've walked a mile down the beach, the sky darkens. Aside from the occasional foredunes, there is nothing but gray ocean and low white sand for as far as I can see. There is no shelter from the approaching storm, and an overwash would mean a long wade back across the flats. Five royal terns stand on the beach facing the freshening breeze, and laughing gulls ride the wind above the dunes. The air cools. I turn around and head back.

The storm holds off, and by the time I reach Portsmouth village, the sky is almost clear, the air heavy and hot. I swat my bare leg and blood splatters across the palm of my hand. A fog of mosquitoes engulfs me. I reach for a small container of Deet, the one item I never leave home without.

Snakes, spiders, and millipedes have never bothered me. I can howl cheerfully with wolves and coyotes and swim contentedly with barracudas and sharks—at least small ones. In general, I enjoy, or at least tolerate, almost all life in the natural world. But mosquitoes are different; mosquitoes I don't like.

I suspect that the marauders attacking me are not ordinary summer mosquitoes but saltwater mosquitoes, *Aedes solicitans*, known in entomological circles as "golden saltmarsh mosquitoes." And the ones biting me are female golden saltmarsh mosquitoes. In almost all of the 2,500 mosquito species in the world, the males drink only nectar from flowers. It's the females that do the damage. They need blood to produce their eggs.

They get it by probing the flesh of warm-blooded animals with tiny stilettos called stylets. When they find a blood vessel, they inject a dab of saliva which contains an anticlotting agent, and then they suck out the blood. Since the average mosquito weighs only $\frac{1}{25,000}$ ounce, you're not likely to feel it on your skin. And by the time the itching starts, the mosquito is usually gone. You can occasionally get lucky with a quick slap, but fighting mosquitoes with your hands is a battle you can't win. To beat these rascals, you must resort to chemical warfare. You must use Deet. Preferably, 100-percent Deet.

Deet is the common name for N,N-diethyl-m-toluamide. Unlike truly nasty chemicals like DDT, Deet doesn't kill mosquitoes (or anything else). It simply blocks the pores in your skin. Since mosquitoes home in on the warm, moist exudate that passes through those pores, an application of Deet confuses them. They'll buzz around you, but since you no longer *smell* edible, they won't bite.

Slathered with the stuff, I make my way back through the deserted village. It took two events to empty this town, to

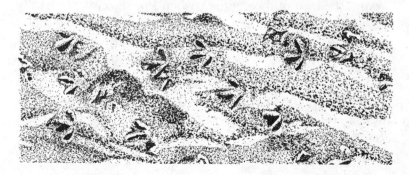

reduce it to this small, nostalgic monument. The first event, the opening of Hatteras Inlet, allowed oceangoing ships to sail directly into Pamlico Sound; since lightering was expensive and dangerous, skippers preferred the new inlet to Ocracoke Inlet. But Portsmouth was still the metropolis of the Outer Banks, and it might have hung on for a while except for the war. The Civil War left the town decimated.

By 1860, the population of Portsmouth had reached 685. In August 1861, Union forces overwhelmed the Confederate fort at Cape Hatteras. A few days later, the Confederates abandoned their fort on Beacon Island in Ocracoke Inlet. With no protection from the Union army, the residents of Portsmouth panicked and evacuated the island. After the war, many did not come back. Those that did found a town whose reason for being was past: ship traffic was almost nonexistent. In 1867, the Treasury Department closed the collector's office in Portsmouth. The population continued to decline. By 1950, only fourteen people called the island home, and twenty-one years later, they, too, were gone. Portsmouth had come full circle.

Precious little remains on the island to remind visitors of the boom years. Most of the structures still standing were built around the turn of this century, when Portsmouth was hardly more than a fishing village. But neither boom nor bust much affected the land. In 1795, when Portsmouth was still a tiny outpost, a surveyor named Jonathan Price wrote the following: "Toward the Ocean, Core banks are sandy and barren, and towards the sound there is a large marsh: small shrubs cover the middle ground, on which are a few farms; but none of them is considerable."

In the mid-nineteenth century, near the peak of the town's

prosperity, Edmund Ruffin described the beach:

> *In the rear of the firm sea-shore . . . lies what I will distinguish as the* sand flat. *This, opposite Portsmouth, is nearly a mile broad, and nearly of uniform plane. . . . The flat very gradually descends . . . and becomes lower and lower, until nearly reaching the range of sand hills. . . . In every storm, the waves . . . pass, in part, over the ridge or highest beach line; and the water thence flows and spreads in a very shallow sheet, over the whole of this lower flat.*

Both passages accurately describe the island today. Except for a few acres in the historic district, Portsmouth is essentially unchanged from its pre-European state. Like the fiddler crabs in the road, the land has survived almost unscathed. Perhaps the periodic storms, the overwashes, and the strong sea winds have swept the usual signs of human wear and tear from the island. Perhaps the early residents simply wrote their histories lighter on the land than we do these days. In any case, the result is a fine and unusual natural area, one as interesting to hikers and naturalists as it is to historians.

On the return trip to Ocracoke, I ask Junius Austin about life on Portsmouth Island when he lived there. Junius is not a talkative man, and the roar of the inboard allows him to politely ignore the question. But when I ask him about the mosquitoes, about how the islanders survived them in the pre-Deet days, his body stiffens and he turns to face me.

"Warn't easy," he says quietly. "Those mosquitoes were mighty rough."

As I said, not much has changed on Portsmouth Island.

Before You Go

For More Information

Cape Lookout National Seashore
3601 Bridges Street, Suite F
Morehead City, N.C. 28557
(919) 728-2121

Accommodations

For lodging in Ocracoke, contact
Greater Hyde County Chamber of Commerce
Engelhard, N.C. 27824

Campgrounds

Camping is permitted in Cape Lookout National Seashore, but there are no developed campsites in the park. Portsmouth Island can be hot and buggy, so if you choose to camp there, select a campsite with a breeze.

The nearest developed campground is on Ocracoke Island. For information, contact
Cape Hatteras National Seashore
Route 1, Box 675
Manteo, N.C. 27954
(919) 473-2111

Maps

There is a good map of Portsmouth village in the national seashore's free brochure, and the route to the beach is well marked. If you plan to explore more of the island, I suggest using a topographic map (USGS: Portsmouth).

Special Precautions

No food, water, or services of any kind are available on Portsmouth Island, and except for the historic area, there is no high ground or shade. In summer, take plenty of water, sunblock, and Deet.

Additional Reading

Fiddler Crabs of the World by Jocelyn Crane, Princeton University Press, Princeton, N.J., 1975.

"The History of Portsmouth North Carolina From Its Founding in 1753 to Its Evacuation in the Face of Federal Forces in 1861" by Kenneth E. Burke, Jr., master's thesis, University of Richmond, 1976.

Mosquitoes by Dorothy Hinshaw Patent, Holiday House, New York, 1986.

The Outer Banks of North Carolina by David Stick, University of North Carolina Press, Chapel Hill, 1958.

Portsmouth Island by Ben B. Salter, self-published, 1972.

"Portsmouth Yesterday and Today" by Joel Arrington, *Wildlife in North Carolina* 48, March 1984, 7–13.

A Survey History of Cape Lookout National Seashore by F. Ross Holland, Jr., Division of History, Office of Archeology and Historic Preservation, National Park Service, Washington, D.C., 1968.

"Village in Limbo" by Franc White, *New East* 1, March/April 1973, 13–15.

Index